The Way to Wholeness:
Stories of Physical, mental, and emotional healing

Tiffany Roberts, Msc.D, DNM, MSHP

Featuring: Gabe Roberts, Msc.D, DC; Nina Hermann, Brooke Silberhorn DC, Courtney Davis DC, James Breeding, Carla Center

Copyright © 2023 The Subconscious Healer Ministry/ Tiffany Roberts ALL RIGHTS RESERVED.
No part of this book or its associated ancillary materials may be reproduced or transmitted in any form or by any means, electronic or mechanical, including photocopying, recording, or by any informational storage or retrieval system without permission from the publisher. PUBLISHED BY: The Subconscious Healer Ministry., DISCLAIMER AND/OR LEGAL NOTICES While all attempts have been made to verify information provided in this book and its ancillary materials, neither the author or publisher assumes any responsibility for errors, inaccuracies or omissions and is not responsible for any financial loss by customer in any manner. Any slights of people or organizations are unintentional. If advice concerning legal, financial, accounting or related matters is needed, the services of a qualified professional should be sought. This book and its associated ancillary materials, including verbal and written training, is not intended for use as a source of legal, medical or financial advice. You should be aware of the various laws governing business transactions or other business practices in your particular geographical location.
EARNINGS & INCOME DISCLAIMER With respect to the reliability, accuracy, timeliness, usefulness, adequacy, completeness, and/ or suitability of information provided in this book, Tiffany Roberts, Gabe Roberts , The Subconscious Healer Ministry, its partners, associates, affiliates, consultants, and/or presenters make no warranties, guarantees, representations, or claims of any kind. Readers' results will vary depending on a number of factors. Any and all claims or representations as to medical advice are not to be considered as average success.. Testimonials are not representative. This book and all products and services are for educational and informational purposes only. Use caution and see the advice of qualified professionals. Check with your medical professional, accountant, attorney or professional advisor before acting on this or any information. You agree that Tiffany Roberts and/or Gabe Roberts and/or The Subconscious Healer Ministry is not responsible for the success or failure of your personal, business, health or financial decisions relating to any information presented by Tiffany Roberts/Gabe Roberts, The Subconscious Healer Ministry., or company products/services. Earnings potential is entirely dependent on the efforts, skills and application of the individual person. Any examples, stories, references, or case studies are for illustrative purposes only and should not be interpreted as testimonies and/or examples of what reader and/or consumers can generally expect from the information. No representation in any part of this information, materials and/or seminar training are guarantees or promises for actual performance. Any statements, strategies, concepts, techniques, exercises and ideas in the information, materials and/or seminar training offered are simply opinion or experience, and thus should not be misinterpreted as promises, typical results or guarantees (expressed or implied). The author and publisher (Tiffany Roberts/ The Subconscious Healer Ministry. (SHMI) or any of SHM's representatives) shall in no way, under any circumstances, be held liable to any party (or third party) for any direct, indirect, punitive, special, incidental or other consequential damages arising directly or indirectly from any use of books, materials and or seminar trainings, which is provided "as is," and without warranties.

Editor: Tanya Vezza
Front and back cover design: Emily Vezza
Front photo credit: Simon Wilkes

A special gift for you, reader:

Grab your free course on the subconscious mind

ULTIMATE SELF-DEVELOPMENT COURSE

https://freegiftfromshm.com/

Deep within the recesses of our mind, Lies a place where troubles we can leave behind, A space where we can rest and heal, And let go of wounds that we can't conceal.

In this realm of dreams and subconscious thought, We find a sanctuary where we can be taught, The secrets of our souls and innermost fears, And learn to let go of our pain and tears.

Here we can explore the depths of our being, And find the answers to the questions we're seeking, We can mend our broken hearts and broken dreams, And find the strength to face life's many extremes.

Through the power of our minds, we can find peace, And our subconscious can guide us to release, The pain that holds us back from our true potential And help us find a way to be truly essential.

So let us enter this sacred space, And let our subconscious take its rightful place, As the guide that will help us heal and grow And find the peace, we need to let our spirits glow.

- Tiffany Roberts

MOTIVATE AND INSPIRE OTHERS!
"SHARE THIS BOOK"
RETAIL PRICE $19.95

Special Quantity Discount

5-20 books	$17.95
21-99 books	$15.95
100-499 book	$10.95
500-999 books	$8.95
1000 + books	$6.95

To place an order contact:
elevateyourfield@pm.me
thesubconscioushealer.com

The Way to Wholeness Intention Statements

May the intention of this book provide you a practical guide to achieving greater emotional, mental, and spiritual balance, and help you discover your unique path to wholeness.

May this book offer insights and tools that will help you overcome personal challenges, heal from past traumas, and connect with your inner selves in a more meaningful way.

May this book inspire you to take responsibility for your own healing and growth, and to empower you to create a life that is aligned with your values and aspirations.

May it help you cultivate self-awareness, self-acceptance, and self-love, and to encourage you to embrace your authentic self.

May it provide a holistic approach to healing and personal transformation, which incorporates the mind, body and spirit, and addresses the root cause of pain and suffering.

This book shares stories of real people who have overcome adversity and found their way to wholeness, and may it inspire you to believe that you too can create positive change in your life.

May it promote a message of hope, resilience, and possibility, and encourage you to embrace the journey to self-discovery and personal growth with courage and curiosity.

May it offer practical strategies and techniques for managing stress, building resilience, and developing healthy habits that support well-being and wholeness.

May it provide you with a roadmap for creating a meaningful and fulfilling life, based on your unique needs, values and goals.

May it create a supportive and compassionate space for you to explore your inner world, connect with others, and discover the joy of living authentically and wholeheartedly.

DEDICATION

*To all those who have ever felt lost, broken, or disconnected from the world around them.
This book is dedicated to you, with the hope that it may serve as a guiding light on your path to wholeness.*

May its words offer comfort, clarity, and inspiration, as you navigate the challenges of life and embark on the journey of self-discovery and personal growth.

May you find within these pages the tools, insights, and encouragement you need to heal from past wounds, overcome present obstacles, and create a brighter future for yourself and those around you.

*And may you know, beyond a doubt, that you are worthy of love, acceptance, and belonging, and that your unique gifts and talents have the power to transform the world in ways both great and small.
With deepest gratitude and respect,*

Tiffany Roberts

THE WAY TO WHOLENESS

A message for you!

Dear Reader,

I am honored and grateful that you have chosen to join me and my colleagues on this journey towards greater wholeness and well-being. Whether you are here because you are seeking healing from past wounds, looking to overcome present challenges, or simply seeking a deeper connection with your inner self, I want you to know that you are not alone.

As you read through the pages of this book, my hope is that you will find within its words a sense of comfort, clarity, and guidance. I hope that it will offer you practical tools and strategies for managing stress, building resilience, and cultivating greater self-awareness and self-acceptance. And I hope that it will inspire you to believe in your own innate strength, wisdom, and capacity for growth and transformation.

Please know that the journey towards wholeness is not always easy, and there may be times when you feel overwhelmed or uncertain. But I want you to know that you are capable of overcoming and obstacle that comes your way, and that every step you take towards greater self-awareness and self-acceptance brings you closer to peace, joy, and fulfillment you deserve.

Thank you for entrusting me with your journey towards wholeness. May this book serve as a source of comfort, support, and inspiration on your path.

With deepest respect and admiration,
Tiffany Roberts

DISCLAIMER

The information presented in this book is intended to provide general guidance and support for individuals seeking to improve their emotional, mental, and spiritual well-being. The authors are not licensed therapist or medical professionals, and the content of this book is not intended to serve as a substitute for professional advice or treatment.

The reader should be aware that the practices and techniques presented in this book may not be suitable for everyone. It is important to use discretion and common sense when applying the information in this book to one's own life, and to consult with a qualified professional before making any significant changes to one's physical or mental health regimen.

The authors are not responsible for any error or omissions in the content of this book, or for any losses, damages, or injuries that may result from the use or misuse of the information presented herein. The reader assumes full responsibility for any actions taken based on the information presented in this book.

The opinions expressed in this book are solely those of the author, and do not necessarily reflect the views or opinions of any organization, institute, or individual mentioned in this book.

By reading this book, the reader acknowledges and accepts the terms of this disclaimer and agrees to use the information presented in this book at their own risk.

Table of contents

Introduction 3

Chapter one: 6
The Journey to Wholeness
Dr Tiffany Roberts, Msc.D, MSN

Chapter two: 14
Holographic Manipulation Therapy
The whole approach to reversing childhood trauma
Dr Gabe Roberts, DC, Msc.D

Chapter Three: 29
Seeking Harmony for a Traumatized World
By James Breeding

Chapter Four: 43
The gift of symptoms and pain
By Dr Courtney Davis, DC

Chapter Five: 62
Finding my Voice: My Healing Journey after a Thyroid Cancer Diagnosis
By Dr Brooke Silberhorn DC

Chapter six: 84
Evolution is an inside job; untangling what doesn't belong to discover true essence within
By Nina Hermann

Chapter seven: 111
From Survival to Freedom
By Carla Center

Chapter eight: 128
Embracing the Journey

INTRODUCTION

Life is full of twists and turns, highs and lows, joys and sorrows. At times, it can be overwhelming, confusing, and downright painful. We all face challenges and obstacles in our lives that can leave us feeling lost, broken, or disconnected from ourselves and the world around us. But amidst the chaos and turmoil of life, there is also a potential for growth, healing, and transformation.

This book, "The Way to Wholeness" is a guide to navigating the journey towards greater emotional, mental, and spiritual well-being. It is a roadmap for those seeking to heal from past wounds, overcome present challenges, and connect with their inner selves in a more meaningful way. It offers insights, tools, and inspiration to help you create a life that is aligned with your values and aspirations, and to help you discover your unique path towards wholeness.

At its core, this book is about the power of self-awareness, self-acceptance, and self-love. It is about learning to embrace your authentic self, with all your strengths and vulnerabilities, and to live your life with purpose, meaning and joy.

In the following pages, we will explore a variety of topics and themes related to personal growth and healing including:

- The importance of self-awareness in creating a fulfilling life
- The role of self-compassion in overcoming obstacles, and strategies for healing.
- The impact of past trauma on our present experiences, and strategies for healing
- The role of relationships in our personal growth and well-being.
- The power of mindfulness in reducing stress and increasing well-being
- Strategies for managing anxiety, depression, and other mental health concerns.
- The importance of physical health and well-being in achieving emotional and mental balance.
- The role of spirituality and connection in our personal growth and healing.

Throughout this book, we will draw on a variety of sources and perspectives, including psychology, spirituality, neuroscience, and personal experience. I will share stories of real people who have overcome adversity and found their way to wholeness, and offer practical strategies and techniques for managing stress, building resilience, and developing healthy habits that support well-being and wholeness.

But perhaps most importantly, I want to convey the message that you are not alone on this journey. No matter what challenges you may be facing, or how lost or broken you feel, there is always hope for healing and growth. You have the power within you to create positive change in your life, and to find the peace, joy, and fulfillment you deserve.

As we embark on this journey towards greater wholeness and well-being, I encourage you to approach this book with an open mind and heart.

Take what resonates with you and leave behind what doesn't. And most importantly, be gentle with yourself along the way. Healing and personal growth are not linear processes, and there will be ups and downs along the way. But with patience, perseverance, and a willingness to embrace the journey, you can create a life that is truly whole and fulfilling.

So let us begin. The journey towards wholeness starts with a single step, and I am honored and grateful to walk this path alongside you.

CHAPTER ONE
The Journey to Wholeness

"I do not limit God by seeing limitation in myself. With God and myself all things are possible." Florence Scovel Schinn

The journey towards wholeness begins with a single step, and for many that step involves accessing the deeper levels of our own mind and harnessing the power of our subconscious to promote healing and growth.

Subconscious healing involves cultivating a deep sense of self-awareness and self-acceptance and learning to access the deeper levels of our own mind to heal from past traumas, overcome present challenges, and create a brighter future for ourselves.

But where do we begin on this journey towards greater wholeness and well-being? What steps can we take to access the power of our own subconscious mind and promote healing and growth?

Cultivate self-awareness
The first step towards subconscious healing is cultivating a deep sense of self-awareness. This involves tuning into our own thoughts, emotions, and behaviors, and gaining insight into our own patterns, motivations and needs.

Imagine if you will that we all have two large dump trucks where we store things. One dump truck is the Divine's dump truck. The other is the dump truck that we store all our negative thoughts, self-talk and negative memories and experiences.

Now the Divine dump truck is nearly empty. There may be a few pebbles in there when we've had happy times, gratitude, and joyful memories. But when it is compared to the negative dump truck it is hardly full.

The negative dump truck is one where we store all the negative talk that goes on inside us each day. For many of us that is a lot of pebbles tossed into the bed of that truck. This is also where the negative moments, memories and experiences are placed.

That negative dump truck is so full for most of us, and it is heavy. It is so heavy that it drags us down making us slower as we drive along. It takes a lot of effort to drive this truck. This is where our illnesses, aches and pains, poor luck and disbelief in ourselves start to manifest.

But it can be changed.

By emptying the negative dump truck one pebble at a time and placing it into the Divine truck, this is where change happens. You see no matter how full this truck gets it is always hauled off and emptied to remain a lighter load.

When we place all the negative events, emotions, thoughts, and experiences into the Divine's truck we are releasing it to God. We surrender it to the Divine and takes it to lighten our load.

At first this is difficult to do, and it seems overwhelming because we have such a huge load to transfer. But eventually that negative load becomes something so easy that we hand it over to God and one day miracles start to happen.

Your life starts to turn direction. You start to become happier. You start to feel better. Anything you want in life just starts to happen and comes so easy.

Before you know it the negative dump truck no longer has a load and is no longer heavy. There is no need for this truck in your life. You begin to see only positive things and turn everything over to the Divine.

This is when life becomes so amazing.

Identifying limiting beliefs
Once you start the process of unloading the dump truck now you become aware of limiting beliefs in yourself.

Limiting beliefs are negative, self-defeating thoughts or attitudes that prevent us from living the life we truly desire.

Common limiting beliefs about our own worth and value, our ability to achieve our goals and our ability to connect with others.

Identifying these limiting beliefs is the step in releasing them and creating new, positive beliefs that support our growth and well-being.

These are the beliefs that hold you back when you have a great idea but then quickly feel that it won't happen, you aren't good enough, it would never happen for you. These are lies we tell ourselves.

These thoughts may have even come from cellular memory from birth.

These thoughts can be eliminated and reframed so that you believe in yourself and limiting beliefs are a thing of the past. You are able to recognize them and quickly shift that way of thinking.

Belief is a major key in anything you want in life. Whether that belief is positive or negative.

Self-compassion
Self-compassion involves treating ourselves with the same kindness, concern, and compassion that we offer a dear friend.

The words, thoughts, and actions you do to yourself daily is something that needs evaluated. If those words or actions were placed on a friend, would you still be friends?

Would you allow someone to speak to your friend the way you speak to yourself? If not, then we need to evaluate why you are speaking to yourself this way. Why are you allowing this to happen to yourself but not a friend?

Positive affirmations
I have found that although for some affirmations are a lifechanging action, for most it is not.

And here is why.

Affirmations are words that are intended to help with positive speak to yourself. However, if your core identity does not match that phrase, then it will fight back with a vengeance.

Affirmations don't work for most because we must address the core identity within ourselves that make us not believe that positive sentence.

Most people quit before the affirmations take hold. It's too hard. Or too much work. I know, I was in the same boat.

But finding the icky feelings that are produced while saying those affirmations, somatically bridging them, deleting those icky feelings from our nervous system then changing the frequency and inserting that positive affirmation into our field is truly powerful.

The key is finding those beliefs and changing them. Not just forcing them on a piece of paper and memorizing it.

Practice gratitude
Gratitude is a super powerful tool for promoting well-being and wholeness. It involves focusing on a positive aspect of our lives and cultivating a sense of appreciation for the good things we have.

Practicing gratitude can help us shift our focus from negative thoughts and emotions and promote greater feelings of joy and contentment.
This is something that I do twice per day even on days I don't feel like it. It is a very powerful thing do to on a regular basis.

By doing this exercise even in the darkest of times you are shifting your frequency to positive. Once this happens the world around you has no choice but to respond to you in positive ways. It is law.

What you give out is what you receive. If you do not give out negative or poor thoughts, it cannot be received. The universe is a mirror of your inner self. If you are grateful all day, it can only give you something to be grateful for.

Visualization
Visualization is a powerful tool for accessing the deeper levels of our own mind and promoting healing and growth.

By visualizing positive outcomes and experiences, we can begin to rewire our subconscious mind and create a new pattern of thought and behavior.

Once you change the negative beliefs within yourself and then you start to visualize you will soon see that the vision will come about.

Forgiveness
Forgiveness is powerful for promoting health and growth. It involves letting go of negative emotions and beliefs that may be holding us back and releasing ourselves from the burden of the past hurts and traumas.

Practicing forgiveness can be a difficult process, but it can ultimately lead to greater emotional and mental well-being. By releasing the negative emotions and beliefs that may be holding us back, we can create space for new, positive experiences and beliefs to enter our lives.

Seek support
Subconscious healing is not a journey we need to take alone. Seeking out support from friends, family members, or professionals can be a powerful tool for promoting healing and growth.

You will find as you read this book that there are several practitioners that are willing to help and have been in similar situations.

Embrace the journey.
Finally, it is important to remember that the journey towards subconscious healing is not a quick fix or one-time event. It is an ongoing process that requires patience, persistence, and a willingness to confront our own fears and vulnerabilities.

But with courage, compassion and a commitment to our own healing and growth, we can tap into the power of our subconscious mind and create a life that is truly whole and fulfilling. We can overcome the wounds of the past, navigate the challenges of the present, and create a brighter future for ourselves and those around us.

Chapter Two
Holographic Manipulation Therapy ™

The Whole Approach to Reversing Adverse Childhood Trauma

Dr Gabe Roberts, DC, DM

My experience comes from over the last decade working with chronically ill people, who suffer from numerous conditions including autoimmune diseases, physiological illnesses, and cancer. I have worked in functional medicine, having a diplomat in nutrition, dozens of certifications in energy medicine, acupuncture, quantum integration as well as a variety of different techniques with the focus of stimulating the body's natural healing systems. This journey of over a decade has led my primary focus to understanding the mind, because the answer to heal is not in another energy treatment, a pill or supplement. Your answer to heal is not in a parasite cleanse or a liver detox herb.

Your key to achieving permeant and dramatic healing in your body always begins with your mind. My focus today is applying the arts and science of Psychosomatic Medicine.

My experience also comes from living though my own traumatic experiences, including being born into a world of substance abuse, physical abuse, emotional neglect which created tremendous pain and distress that followed me for years, despite my best efforts to mask the pain. These included years of drug use myself, being associated with the worse of the worse crowd, criminal activities and eventually to attempt at getting a clean slate from all of this, joining the Marine Corps and completing several oversea combat tours.

The day I was born, my father was drunk and passed out unconscious on the floor when my mother went into labor. My uncle had to literally kick him on the ground yelling at him to "Wake up, your wife is going into labor!" Knowing what I know now about how the earliest experience shape the brain, including in the womb, it is no wonder why I spent so much of my early life in "fight or flight" mode. My brain centers were formed while I lived in threating conditions.

Looking back, I only remembered days of living in fear, as my stepfather was always intoxicated, extremely violent and carried some of his own biases and traumas he was acting out, a trait that is passed down in nearly every family. As a child who experienced fear, physical beatings from him and a mother who was emotionally absent, it was no wonder by the time I had any chance, I was engaging in substance abuse, including smoking marijuana, drinking alcohol, and engaging in harder street drugs-all as a way of numbing the pain. Any type of engagement in using drugs, whether it is alcohol, narcotics, marijuana or even prescriptions, are usually tied in one way or another as an attempt to dull pain.

It is important to understand that emotional pain and physical pain are felt in the same identical areas of the brain. So, emotional rejection stimulates the same area in the neurology as stepping on a nail.

By the time I was a teenager, I was so engaged into drugs, that I barely graduated high school and even spent time in jail for illegal drug use. This of course was all unintentional, but I was unconsciously seeking out what was most familiar to my psyche, or the earliest and most powerful memories. I was looking for a way, without knowing it, to maintain the emotional states from which I was born into and keep myself emersed only in what felt "normal."

When I was 20 years old, I hit rock bottom and decided to abandon everything at an attempt to becoming something else. Never knowing my father growing up, and only having an emotionally absent, drunken stepfather as the only male figure I was ever around, I intuitively knew that I wanted to be around someone with true leadership qualities. Someone who was above all that I had known, so I made the decision to join the Marines and leave the part of the country I grew up in.

Of course, this engaged me with leaders and allowed me to meet influential people who helped me become more then I was, but the pain was always still there.

Years later, I even became a doctor looking to find out what to do about this underlying, deep relentless pain that was hidden and not even on the radar of any academic studies I engaged in. No one in all my educational curriculum ever mentioned the subconscious, other than as a part that regulates the heart and digestion and other autonomic functions.

This only came to me when I began studying the effects of repressed emotions, traumatic impacts effect on the body, and focusing on a psychosomatic approach which is what completely dissolved a lifetime of pain.

Psyche, meaning the soul is also another name for your subconscious mind and soma, meaning the physical body and all the primordial substance that your body is comprised of, and this is the basic definition begin the meaning of psychosomatic. I once believed that all diseases began in the gut, but this is not true. All diseases begin in the mind. If you have chaotic thoughts or conflict in your subconscious, which is typically from traumatic overwhelm during childhood years, the body will manifest this and the impact of acupuncture, nutritional supplements and regular exercise will not necessarily resolve this conflict.

Conflict in the mind is the causative factor in most diseases, self-sabotaging behaviors, and addictions, as it was in my life as well. Smoking marijuana was the activity I most engaged in to escape the pain which was boiling down below. Even the famous Rolling Stones guitarists Keith Richards said something that concurs with this, from his years of being a heroin addict. "All the contortions we put ourselves through, just not to be ourselves for a few hours" is indicative of drug use (or other distractive behaviors) are all attempts to get away from pain.

This means that you can, unintentionally be addicted to drugs and eventually develop disease, by having conflicts and your deepest pockets of your mind, that are beyond your conscious understanding or awareness.

Today, my professional focus is to help alleviate, assist, and treat by successfully reversing a host of physiological illnesses, mystery symptoms, chronic pain, autoimmune conditions, addictive behaviors and more which all have at their root cause, repressed emotions.

The focus of our approach is primarily on memories, traumatic overwhelming encoded moments that are captured in the millisecond of overwhelm, stored when our nervous system snaps a picture through the five senses, and immediately stores this moment of overwhelm in any of our body's neurons throughout our nervous system. This was the source

and the mechanism of the pain I carried through most of my life, and with Holographic Manipulation Therapy ™, it is now completely gone.
It is important to understand that when it comes to the factors that compromise your health and happiness, or the physical well-being of your body, the problem is very simple. It's not the past that is haunting us. It's how the body and the mind store the past. That is the real issue.

Although this is not well known by most professionals in the healing arts, one of the biggest factors that compromises our health is that we have the remarkable ability to freeze the flow of consciousness when we are overwhelmed with an experience.

Our neurology can instantaneously "pause" the flow of consciousness when you are at the peak of neurological arousal, momentarily holding the breath and snap a photograph of everything your senses are picking up and store the entire quantum perception in any of your neurons. This encoded memory becomes the nagging back pain or neck pain that doesn't completely disappear after a massage or a chiropractic adjustment.

As a chiropractor, I know from clinical experience that most of people's ongoing pain is not from segmental displacements in your vertebrae column, but it is stored memories.

Dr John Sarno, MD is one who was fully aware of this type of phenomena that occurred in his patients and as I have begun to focus on repressed emotions, traumatic memories and releasing moment of overwhelm in my patients, I too have witnessed chronic pain disappear and never return. Stored memory is that powerful. It becomes the lump in the throat, the weight on the shoulders, the vice on the head, the nausea that arises when the person is very nervous and the aches in the jaw when any frustrations are triggered.

The way that these memories are stored are how the past is encoded in your neurology is what creates a series of health challenges in people on numerous ways.

First, your memories are recorded as holographic imprints which are 3 dimensional and composed of millions of fragments of light particles. Each individual light particle is holographic, or holonomic, meaning behaves like a hologram, and each light particle contains the entire memory and every detail of exactly what happened. If you encounter anything similar to what was encoded, a fragment of the memory is triggered and suddenly the entire memory returns to our neurological awareness.

Ever know someone who is "stuck" in a fight or flight type of condition? It is because their subconscious mind does not know the treat or overwhelming circumstance is over yet, even if their conscious mind is fully aware that it has passed. Secondly, we are trance machines, constantly going in and out of a hypnosis like state day in and day out. Think about this for a moment. Driving a car down the road, waiting in line at a supermarket, walking down the sidewalk on a nice day are all examples of simple things we do on a regular basis without being aware of how often or how many times we gaze off, leaving the present moment and revisiting past memories.

Our mind drifts into previous memories anywhere from 15 to 50 times per hour, and this is just a normal part of how our mind works. If those memories that come up into our awareness have an imprint of anything threatening, like a scene from the TV, an argument we had with a loved one, being late to work or anything else that is perceived as a threat by the nervous system, our HPA axis and adrenal system immediately responds by activating the fight or flight system.

This combination of reliving previous memories, with the nervous system reacting as if the memories are still presently going on in real time, is the most significant contributor on why people are often plagued with chronic pain, autoimmune conditions and worse, even if they are living healthy lives on the surface.

The third factor to understand is that according to research performed by Mihaly Csikszentmihalyi, your unconscious mind forms 99.994% of your overall awareness and your conscious mind is 0.006%.

This means that the thoughts that you are aware of and the thoughts that you are thinking about right now, make up less than a thousandth of your overall awareness and this tiny part is what most of us are convinced is in charge.

The conscious mind is largely dominated by deeper centers of the brain which regulate feelings and impulse control, so it is these deeper systems that are responsible for controlling your life. By the time you have a conscious thought, that data has already been run through countless lenses, your identity or self-image (formed at ages 0-6 years old), several apertures and two other fundamental sections of your brain before finally becoming something that you are aware of. In other words, your thoughts and conscious awareness has been watered down and skewed, in a large part, by early experiences from childhood.

Imagine you are walking outside on a dirt road and suddenly see something that makes you jump in fear. Your nervous system, within nanoseconds, believes there is a snake on the ground causing your heart to suddenly jump, your muscles to react and you instantly leap back to only realize that what you saw is just a rope on the ground that resembled a snake.

Now ask yourself what happened?

The information that came into your eyes, were instantly interpreted by your unconscious brain center's that have first dibs on all information. Before you even had a rational thought or idea of what was going on, your body reacted and you physically jumped back, to only realize "Oh, it's just a rope."

Your conscious mind was the last part of you to realize this and by then the other, more powerful parts of your mind had already initiated a response long before you had a conscious thought of what was happening. This is how it happens with every incident you come across in life, whether you are aware of it or not.

Now that you are aware of how your mind is orientated, it is important to understand that we will only conform to what those earliest brain centers commands are. In terms of how this applies to health and wellness, is that if you have an identity that doesn't match health, or it believes that "I don't deserve to feel good" or "I am worthless" or "I don't matter" you are only going to achieve a level of health that conforms to this command.

Your identity, or self-image, is one of the most powerful lenses of how you see yourself and this is anchored into these deep centers of the brain that has first dibs on the information. In every patient we've ever met, had an identity that did not reflect deserving of health. Remember, although this is all going on below the surface of conscious awareness. Every cell in the person's body is eavesdropping on this kind of message, even if they were taking the best supplements and eating whole, organic food.

You cannot override the signal of a poor self-image by attempting to live a healthy lifestyle. A woman who came to us with chronic Lyme condition for over 8 years had every symptom disappear and never return when we helped her transform her identity from "I deserve to suffer" to "I deserve vibrant health and happiness." Why? Her self-image matched health and her body was no longer vulnerable to the cyclic illness brought on by the bacterial infection.

If you are going to have real changes in your health, your physical well-being, your income and influence the deepest most powerful parts of your nervous system to heal your physical body, you must get the deepest centers involved. This is where the technology of Holographic Manipulation Therapy (HMT) ™ comes in.

HMT ™ is a client focused process which facilitates the complete removal of the traumatic encoded memory and therefore proves to the 99.994% subconscious mind that the event is over. It is not hypnosis but is more accurately described as getting you out of a hypnotic trance, which, is what a traumatic event does to your mind.

The capabilities it has can pinpoint the earliest moment of trauma, including ones from in the womb, childhood, or ancestorial memories and disarm the holographic conflicts, memory imprints and therefore allows the body to fully facilitate the healing and repair mechanisms which are inhibited when the nervous system is in a constant state of alarm, a consequence that happens with adverse childhood experiences.

HMT ™ provides a bridging point, allowing a "language" for us to dialogue with the 99.994% (Which doesn't use any type of words) and allows us to turn the deepest pockets of conflict or chaos into harmony. It allows these changes to take place in the highly unconscious brain centers (that have first dibs on the information, as we discussed earlier) so our neurology has a signal of peace, harmony, connection and love — even if we were raised in traumatic conditions.

Using HMT ™ on my earliest memories has allowed me to fully heal from all pain, the PTSD and the unconscious distress that followed me for nearly 40 years, disappeared after everything else I attempted provided minimal results.

There is nothing I've ever studied or experienced that compares to the level of trauma clearing HMT ™ provides. It does this by locating the very first and most powerful overwhelming memory, usually from between the ages of 0 to 6 years old, cancels out the frequencies of the entire holographic memory and honors the mechanism of the memory itself, so the nervous system fully allow the releasing of the memory.

What does that mean?

Let's say for example that with the specific memory, there is a lesson or an encoded message that the subconscious mind wants you to hold onto from that experience. If you clear the memory without extracting this message, or "safety lesson", the neurology will resist letting the memory clear and it will come back. Another scenario that happens is that while trying to clear the traumatic memory, a part of the unconscious does not want the memory cleared, or it wants to hold onto something from that memory.

If you try to clear the memory that it wants to hold onto, the neurology will resist the changes and the memory will return, complete with all the unwanted symptoms. These are reasons why many people do change work, as I have myself, and they will get some level of change, but before long, the memory and the symptoms return. This is what makes HMT ™ different and places it as the golden standard for reversing the negative impact of traumatic memories and adverse childhood experiences.

The Practice
I want to share with you the Emotional Motivation Checklist. Everyone has these. think of something you want and be selfish about it. What is it something you want? A desired monthly income, or you want for healing of a health condition. Use this for whatever it is you want. As you look at this, I want you to think about it, even close your eyes and really think about that for a moment. What is that you really, really want?

Now when you look at what you really want in your mind, ask yourself this question. What is important about that? Jot down the answer that comes right to you. On a different line write your next response of what is important about that? Then on a third line you write the answer to what is important about that, each time digging deeper and using different answers. Write down what comes up first, don't edit it or over think it.

Here's the power in this: when you ask your neurology any question, it's going to give you an answer. It'll pop up within 3 seconds and whatever first pops up is the answer you write down. What's important about that? Suddenly, things just start coming up to your mind. Quickly jot them down. Immediately, more answers come to your mind. This format forces your unconscious mind to pipeline into deeper and deeper answers that will change your physical state when you say them out loud. Understand, it is important to say what you want out loud, then repeat all the answers five times out loud as to why it is important to you to get this.

Biography

Dr Gabe Roberts is the Co-Founder of Holographic Manipulation Therapy ™ and is a specialist of psychosomatic illnesses including autoimmune conditions, chronic pain, chronic fatigue, digestive illnesses, neurological conditions, depression and a host of mystery conditions that have at their root cause repressed emotions. He has extensive experience working with patients from around the world helping them resolve their body's health challenges by reconciling conflict in their unconscious mind. Dr Roberts is a Holographic Manipulation Therapist ™, Clinical Hypnotherapist, NLP Practitioner, Self-Sabotage Coach, Quantum Integration Practitioner, has a Doctorate in Metaphysics, he holds a Doctorate in Chiropractic and is Certified in Functional Medicine.

https://thesubconscioushealer.com/

Chapter Three
Seeking Harmony for a Traumatized World
By James Breeding

"Simply dare to assume you are what you want to be and you will compel everyone to play their part." - Neville Goddard

My name is James Breeding and I have been working with clients one on one since 2020. I guess you could say it is in my blood, my mother and father were both Neuro Linguistic Programming (NLP) Master Practitioners. My mother has spent three decades as a family system and substance abuse therapist. I grew up hearing about NLP and the Enneagram while attending conferences with them.

My first entry way into the holistic healing space was a chance meeting with Jason Christoff a Self-Sabotage Coach at a conference in Mexico. He spoke about the power of the subconscious mind and how our own brain is instrumental in sabotaging our success in life.

Frankly, I was dumbfounded that this wasn't common knowledge for most everyone. How many people are frustrated with their lot in life and clueless as to how to change it? I would say 99% of the population has no idea why they operate the way they do.

This small taste of knowledge led me to read voraciously and then finally go through Jason

Christoff's Self Sabotage Coach certification program. I worked with clients for a while and enjoyed educating them on the virtually untapped capacity of the subconscious mind.

It wasn't enough as I wanted to help people make permanent changes to their habits after educating them why they behave the way they do. I was turned on to Psych-K by another coach, so I attended the Basic and master's classes. This provided more depth to really help my clients make lasting changes.

Psych-K is a great modality, but it left me wanting for a more targeted approach to help clients. I felt like I was chipping away at my client's belief systems but unable to make major changes. Clients would report some progress but not the earth-shattering changes I wanted to see for them.

Again, I searched for a modality that would help my clients make wholesale changes to their belief system. I happened upon Conversational Hypnosis and started using it my practice. This was the therapy made popular by the hypnotic legend Milton Erikson. He was capable of putting clients into a trance just by staring at them or saying one word.

Conversational Hypnosis is very effective at untying unconscious knots. Even though it works well it can leave the therapist at a loss as to what happened during the session. The therapist is there to guide the client as they figure out their own solutions to problem.

Even though great success was had with resolving deep seated issues, I still longed for a more targeted therapy as I was exploring helping people with chronic pain relief. As I delved more into chronic pain and the many conditions under the chronic pain umbrella, I started to see the primary role of trauma in most health conditions.

As I was marketing my business on social media, I happened upon the work of Dr. Gabe Roberts. I read over his posts showing the role of trauma and specific health conditions. I was frankly blown away by this new to me thought process.

All my life I had been programmed to believe that every disease could be blamed on invisible bugs, genetics, and happen stance. What if God had provided another way for us to heal?

Intuitively, this made sense to me. The cutting, burning, and poisoning as a solution to health "problems" intuitively never felt right. Masking over conditions with a pill in perpetuity solves nothing. Drug companies are aware of the primary knobs that its drug is turning in the body, but what about the long-term side effects that it is unaware of. We are told by health authorities that this is the only way to health.

As we have seen recently, the "authorities" will do virtually anything to maintain the conventional medicine narrative. Censoring speech, banning natural substances, outlawing proven treatments. This only strengthened my resolve to find another way to help people help themselves through mental and physical health challenges.

After reading several posts by Dr. Roberts, I began to take an interest in the form of therapy he practiced, called Holographic Manipulation Therapy (HMT). The name itself sounded mysterious. What do holograms have to do with helping people overcome traumatic memories?

I soon enrolled in his program to become a certified HMT therapist. This program opened up a whole new world of thought as to how memories are stored in the body. How trauma affects the nervous system. How health conditions seemingly arise out of nowhere. How our past alters our present.

HMT was the tool I was looking for to truly help my clients overcome a myriad of mental and physical health challenges.

HMT involves targeting body sensations that come to surface when we experience uncomfortable feelings. These feelings or sensations are tied to emotionally overwhelming memories that we have long forgotten. The memories may be decades old but as a result of the impact on our psyche they are omnipresent in our lives.

HMT is laser focused on reducing and eliminating these unpleasant memories. These memories form the foundation of our belief system. When negative beliefs are created by a childhood experience, they alter the course of our life. Using HMT, we eliminate and/or re-frame these memories and actively change our belief system.

You could call it belief hacking. Substantially faster and more effective than affirmations and other modalities. The shortcut to getting the life you want versus living out your childhood programming.

With this newfound tool, I decided I wanted to branch out from working strictly with self-sabotage type issues. After researching many niche type issues I decided I wanted to work with women and chronic pain.

Chronic pain is at epidemic levels in the United States. An estimated 50 million people suffer with chronic pain with back, hip, knee, and foot pain being the most common complaint. It is the number one reason people go to see a doctor. It is also the reason for tens of billions of dollars of lost productivity in the economy.

In her 1943 book *Psychosomatic Diagnosis*, Helen Flanders Dunbar made that point that traditional medicine had conquered all the acute diseases of the day while chronic diseases accounted for most deaths in the United States at the time. At the time of writing half of all patient hospital days were devoted to chronic illness.

She predicted chronic illness would explode over the coming decades which turned out to be quite accurate. While some progress has been made with chronic illnesses such as cardiovascular disease since the 1940s, chronic pain has seen very little advancement in terms of curative methods.

Chronic pain is defined as any pain that lasts longer than three months. It often occurs in addition to the pain of the original condition that started it. The original condition may have healed, or it may not have healed. Either way the pain persists independently of the original injury or illness.

Illnesses such as Fibromyalgia fall under the chronic pain category. Fibromyalgia as a defined condition has been around since the 1980s when the term was coined by Rheumatologists. Thousands of studies have been conducted as to the causative factors behind Fibromyalgia with little to no success.

Fibromyalgia patients experience widespread pain in their arms, legs, and trunks. Anxiety, depression, IBS and many other symptoms can accompany this condition. It is often considered a last resort diagnosis after every other condition has been excluded.

Common experiences for fibromyalgia patients are months to years of testing before an actual diagnosis. This period of time is basically used to exclude every other possible condition such as arthritis. Patients report this process as draining, expensive, and stressful.

Once the patients have endured this mentally torturous process, they are labeled with the fibromyalgia diagnosis. At first, getting a diagnosis is a relief after this long process but it doesn't last long. I think the relief comes from the medical testing process coming to an end. Once a patient receives this diagnosis, they are presented with few treatment options.

Pain medications are prescribed to mask the pain, anti-depressants to mask the anxiety, injections, physical therapy, and counseling. As is often with conventional medicine treatment, the symptoms are treated not the root cause. As a result, the condition will most likely persist for the rest of the patient's life.

Throughout the months or years of testing that the average patient endures the mind and body connection are ignored as doctors search for a physical cause for the pain. What I see as "the elephant in the room" is that patients and doctors both ignore is the role of trauma.

Chronic pain patients have experienced trauma at more than twice the rate of the average person. How can this be ignored? We are programmed in Western society to look to conventional medicine to cure or treat every condition in the body. Credit should be given to the amazing advancements medical science has achieved in treating acute injuries and illnesses over the last hundred years or so.

Sadly, those same advancements have not translated into better treatments for chronic illness. With chronic illness on the rise, we have to look beyond the traditional bounds of western medicine.

When I see a society of people that are becoming medical annuities with no hope in sight, I know we are missing something. The role of the mind in the treatment of chronic physical illness should come first not last. Once an acute diagnosis has been ruled out, treatment should immediately shift to the mind body connection.

Chronic pain patients often hear or infer from their doctor is that the pain is all in their head and doesn't exist. The doctors after being unable to find anything physically wrong, are at a loss. Conventional medical thinking is the patient is exaggerating the pain for drugs, monetary gain, or avoidance of responsibility.

Clearly this is not the best approach. As many chronic pain patients have been scarred by this mentality, they mistake the mention of Mindbody healing as the same discounting of their pain that their doctor inferred. When talking with chronic pain patients I must use precise and empathetic language to avoid the triggering of their past treatment experiences.

The physical pain is real, but the source of the pain lies in the unconscious mind or psychosomatic in nature. The problem with this "diagnosis" as Dr. John Sarno, author of *The Divided Mind* found, is that only 10-15% of patients are willing to accept it. In my experience I can't say what the actual percentage is but it still amazes me how many people just refuse to accept this fact.

This is the social stigma of mental health where you can be perceived as "defective" and not someone to associate with. Mental health patients have a long history of being segregated from society and treated horribly.

Although we are making progress against this unfortunate history, the stigma is still alive and well today. Many people consciously avoid mental health work as they feel ashamed and broken. Also, unconsciously their mind views mental work as dangerous and something to be avoided.

In the United States with our "get it done" attitude it can make you appear weak or vulnerable. This is not going to change anytime soon but in the meantime, I can help influence my clients that trauma resolution should be at the top of the list for physical health.

As I learn more about the mind body connection, and how the unconscious mind can physically communicate via the body, I am reminded of another love of mine, permaculture. Permaculture is an ethical design science that emphasizes working with nature instead of against it. Large, degraded landscapes have been rejuvenated in just a few years using this design methodology.

The designer studies the land and all the influences upon it such as the sun, wind pattern, rainfall, animal patterns and so forth. After careful observation over a period of time, the designer creates a design that works with all the elements that impact the land. After implementation, the land actually rejuvenates itself with little human intervention.

Permaculture and holistic healthcare have the same core ethic that you don't impose a treatment or design. You listen to the patient, and you observe what the patient or landscape is communicating to find a treatment that works with the body or land. In Permaculture, if you impose a design without following this design principle you create all kinds of unintended consequences. It is no different in healthcare, when conventional medicine imposes a solution (pills, surgery, etc.) without listening or observing the whole body which leads to all kinds of unintended consequences.

To draw on another analogy, Nassim Nicholas Taleb wrote an article titled the "The Black Swan of Cairo." The article spoke about the Arab Spring that began in early 2011. It detailed how Middle Eastern dictators attempted to suppress the volatile emotions of their population while inflation was running rampant. They tried the usual techniques of threats, imprisonment, and censorship to maintain their grip on power. The end result was several dictators and governments fell during this time. The universal lesson here is that when you try to control volatility you end up with more volatility in the end.

The body operates the same way. When you try to suppress what needs to be expressed, the body reaches a point where it can no longer suppress it. Repressed emotions linger below the surface causing incremental damage until they can no longer be ignored.

Chronic pain is emotional volatility that needs to be expressed in a sense. I help my clients express it by reframing the traumatic moment and defusing the toxic emotions around it. The nervous system releases the tension that has built up over many years and begins to relax. The raging fire that was to come later in life has been extinguished.

German New Medicine is a topic I am learning more about that is based on the principle of unresolved conflicts causing disease in the body. When the disease surfaces, the patient is already in the healing phase. This is a one hundred and eighty degree turn from the Western view of healthcare. As you can imagine, this is not a popular topic with conventional medicine but an amazing holistic tool to understand what the body is trying to communicate. In fact, the practice of German New Medicine is banned in France. In time I hope to fully integrate this learning into my practice.

Along with learning new modalities, it is vitally important to me that when I work with a client, we don't leave any stone unturned. I want them to have a permanent resolution or pathway to it, for whatever issue they came in with. Of course, I am not in control as it's up to the client to be engaged, but my goal is for clients to have life altering changes every time we meet.

I have created my practice with the sole mission of helping women overcome their chronic pain or greatly reduce it. So many women are suffering unnecessarily when the tools are available to end their suffering.

Like I mentioned previously, we face an uphill battle as most people are unable to accept Psychosomatic diagnosis, but I feel the tide is turning as more people grow frustrated with conventional medicine. The awareness of trauma's role in chronic pain is also becoming more widespread.

Women are traumatized over and over again as they go through the medical system enduring invasive tests, medication with side effects, and unempathetic doctors. Suffering with trauma already, this adds another layer of negative beliefs that drives fear and stress which of course increases their physical pain.

How much money will they spend over a lifetime, how many medication side effects will they have to contend with, while still having no long-term relief?

My goal is to educate and empower women to sidestep what I believe is barbaric treatment for a traumatized person. I enjoy watching clients recover from decades of pain after some of them had lost hope. As I continue to help women heal themselves, I thank God for this opportunity.

James Breeding lives with his wife and two kids in Colorado Springs, Colorado. He holds a BBA from the University of North Texas. He spent several decades in the tech industry but wanted to  work with people versus machines. He has obtained education as a Jason Christoff Self Sabotage Coach, Psych-K Master Facilitator, Conversational Hypnotist, and Holographic Manipulation Therapist. He is currently pursuing a Masters in Holistic Healing from Psychosomatic University.

James is the owner of Overcome Self Sabotage LLC. James specializes in helping people overcome chronic pain through Mindbody modalities. Conditions such as back pain, fibromyalgia, IBS, and migraines stand no chance against the power of the unconscious mind. James is passionate about helping clients obtain quick relief that have suffered for years with chronic conditions. His clients have often gone through years of conventional medicine testing and treatment with very little relief to show for it. His goal is to help end chronic pain for as many people as possible while spreading the word of Psychosomatic Medicine. He provides a safe and gentle environment to release trauma and repressed emotions that are at the root of most chronic pain.

James enjoys spending time with his family, hiking, weightlifting, and Permaculture.

Jamesbreeding.com

Chapter Four
The gift of symptoms and pain
Dr Courtney Davis DC

"And we know that in all things God works for the good of those who love him, who have been called according to his purpose."

Romans 8:28 NIV

What if we viewed our pain as a gift? What if it could give you vital information about yourself? What could it be that your pain is trying to tell you? Can you remember your first memories of pain or symptoms?

Is it possible your symptoms and pain could be a roadmap or a red flag trying to get your attention? Trying to tell you things are off course. Trying to tell you your lifestyle choices are needing a major shift?

What if pain and symptoms were not the evil nuisance we have been taught to believe? Not something to instantly drug away and push down and just get rid of? What if they were a gift? What if they were God's direct communication with us telling us where we need to correct our course?

What if pain was a feedback mechanism trying to expose a physical, chemical, or emotional trauma in our body and it was meant to give us feedback on how to better care for our body and ourselves? What if symptoms could be guiding us to where we need to give our attention in our life? What if we leaned into our pain and our symptoms and we listened? Could pain be a key that shifts our minds into the present by triggering a curiosity that demands us to fully feel and experience wholeness.

What if we gave attention to what our body was desperately trying to communicate with us? What if instead of numbing our pain with the vice of choice we paused and gave it a chance to speak to us? What if our pain was there to teach us something we need to know? What if we took a moment to be curious and question our symptoms and their presence? What if the power of pain could be harnessed and used for our good? What if it was meant to be used for healing?

My pain and symptoms began early in life. Now in my early 40's I look back and desperately wish I had someone who could have taught me as a child how to listen to what the symptoms were trying to tell me. Someone who could have helped me understand how to lean in and listened to my body for feedback and direction. I know now it is part of my mission to be able to be this person for others and help them avoid needless suffering.

Stomach pain and nausea are my first and most dominant memories of pain and symptoms. I have very vivid memories as a young 6-year-old girl spending many nights laying on the cold tile bathroom floor in overwhelming nausea waiting desperately for the next wave of throwing up to be over. My intense stomach aches happened up to a few times a week and almost always came on in the middle of the night.

I would wake up urgently with horrible stomach pain feeling scared and lonely. The house would be dark and quiet, and everyone would be asleep. I remember trying not to wake anyone and that I would face the pain alone.

I would quietly run to the bathroom and close the door. I would try to make myself as cozy as possible by grabbing a towel from the towel rack and using the bathroom mat as a bed and then just try to rest through the nausea and pain and wait for the waves of stomach emptying to end.

After 2-5 hours my stomach would be completely empty, and I would be so relieved I could finally crawl back into my cozy bed and go back to sleep. I had so many sleepless nights thinking why is this happening? Looking back, I can see that my body was obviously trying to warn me.

My body was trying to help me. I did not understand how to listen to my symptoms for feedback and information like I do now. Looking back, I can't help but think that if I had listened to the clues and had stopped eating ALL dairy I would have been able to avoid years of needless agony.

When my episodes began, I was seen by my doctor. He had told my parents and me that I was lactose intolerant. He said I should limit eating dairy and that I should be just fine. He said I may possibly soon grow out of it. I was never told to cut dairy out of my diet completely.

Being so young this was hard for me to be aware of and limit. I did not always realize certain things had dairy in them. I could get away with having a little bit, but it accumulated and if I had too much in a few days my body sent me into a purge to clear the toxin it was being exposed to.

These midnight experiences as a child lit a fire in me. It created a desire in me to bring comfort and care into the world. I wanted to prevent the suffering I was going through from happening elsewhere.

Since I had no real tools to help myself with my own symptoms and pain I began to research how to comfort and take care of animals. I felt so much joy in learning to care for animals. I would find birds, bunnies, tadpoles in my backyard that were hurt or without their mom and decide that I needed to build them a safe habitat to be cared for.

I went to the library and checked out every book on caring for animals and pets I could find. I was able to convince my parents to let me get a few pets to care for regularly. We had family dogs and cats but

I also saved my money and got a variety of animals. I had bunnies, birds, fish, and gerbils.

As I got older, I knew I wanted to shift my caregiving to people but particularly children. I knew very early I wanted to be a mom and I wanted to learn everything I could to be the best caregiver I could. I knew deep down that the symptoms I was going through were not normal and there had to be a better way to live. I just knew this was not all God had for me. I was going to figure it out and make sure my children could be healthier than I was.

From 7-13 years old I was around many injuries being a competitive gymnast and I had been conditioned to take a pill at the first sign of a muscle ache or headache. At 13 years old I would carry pain relievers in my purse just in case. I did not ever want to be somewhere without my pain relievers in case I had a pain I needed to extinguish.

I was taught to fear pain. You see, back then I had no awareness of the good pain could teach me. Pain was my villain that slowed down the day. It stole hours away from busyness, from practicing or training in the gym, and made me less able to perform, achieve, study, work or have fun. It robbed me of nights of sleep, and eventually even pursuing my college gymnastic dreams.

By 13 years old I had to give up gymnastics due to the pain of a genetic knee condition I was experiencing. I had Osgood-Schlatter and the only solution I was given was to rest it. My knee pain increased with use which made keeping up with my gymnastic training schedule too painful to maintain.

I became upset with my body and its pain and had no idea how to care for it and respect it. I ran my body ragged and then was confused when it showed symptoms and pain, all warnings that I did not recognize as signs that my body was not keeping up with the demands. Now I understand these symptoms were a red flag, part of my innate feedback, my "engine light" coming on that I did not see, and I kept on driving until my body gave out.

The chiropractor in me wonders if I had supported my body through my training with regular chiropractic care how things could have been different for my gymnastics career. I had not yet learned about the many benefits of chiropractic at that time in my life and was never made aware it was a supportive option. When I was given the knee diagnosis, just like when I was given the stomach diagnosis, I was not recommended to pursue any therapies or receive any help for my knee. I was again told to wait it out and that I should grow out of it.

For the second time in my childhood, I was left with a, this can't be it, feeling. I knew God had more possibilities out there for us. I could not imagine in my childhood world where it seemed there were so many innovations and technologies all around me that there was no one who could give any helpful solutions. It just seemed like something was missing. I knew I was meant to be able to express health better, but I just did not know how.

In high school I enjoyed taking as many biology and science classes as I could. I was on my mission to figure out health, the body and pain. I voiced this interest to a few teachers, and they suggested I consider studying physical therapy. When I got an assignment to pick a profession to job shadow for a day, I quickly picked physical therapy at their recommendation. I was so excited to participate in this day.

I vividly remember showing up and being so let down that it was not what I imagined it would be. I had an instant solid sense I would need to keep searching for what my profession would be. I turned to the internet. I started reading job descriptions online and that is when I found my first calling to chiropractic.

I came across the chiropractic job description and felt something click. I had an instant solid feeling that this was going to be my profession. It sounded like it would teach me the natural health methods I was yearning for.

I had zero experience with chiropractic at this point in my life. I had never been to or even met a chiropractor, but the description had hooked me. It magnetized me and I followed it. I decided from that moment I would study the pre-med classes in college so I could eventually go to chiropractic school.

I entered college ready and eager to study and learn all I could about biology and God's creation and design. I quickly learned that my view of the miracle of life created by God was the minority.

Professors quickly talked down the idea of creation or organized design and presented life as a lucky accident and random chance of cell clustering. It felt like something was missing again and I felt there had to be more than this. I worked through the 4 long years knowing they were just a steppingstone to get me where I needed to be.

While I was in college, I had a significant car accident and ended up with whiplash and a concussion. I was having debilitating neck pain and constant headaches. My dad suggested I go see a chiropractor. I went on his suggestion, and I had my first experience with chiropractic.

As I listened and learned about my body from the chiropractor I wondered where this had been all my life. Why did I have to wait to have a car accident injury to experience chiropractic? I spent the next 8 months rehabbing my injury receiving adjustments and massage. I was so grateful to get a first-hand experience in what I had already decided to go to school for.

When I finally made it to chiropractic school, I felt a huge sense of belonging. I recall sitting in class learning chiropractic philosophy for the first time. We were learning the value of removing interference in the body and restoring function so that the body can express its full God given potential and be more connected to its energy source and God.

We were learning about above, down, inside out, and how chiropractic helps move the life energy from above to flow down more freely and inside our bodies to be expressed outward as health. This was the first time I sat in a class where the miracle of life seemed truly valued. As the months went on, I knew I was in the right place and where God had called me to be. This was part of my mission to someday share with the world.

The more I learned in Chiropractic school the more I felt like the view the world had taught me about pain and symptoms was a lie. I was conditioned and taught that we should, as quickly as possible: disassociate, numb, ice away, push down, run from, avoid and surgically cut out anything that causes pain. There is no need to ever have pain because well you can just take something for it.

Now I was learning how symptoms and pain were a vital part of the feedback mechanism of our nervous system. That symptoms have the ability to give us invaluable information and clues to learn from, not just ignore. I could not believe I had missed out the first half of my life on these lessons pain was trying to teach me.

As my eyes were being opened, I wished I had learned just even the basics of this knowledge as a child. I started to dream about a childhood where I was aware of the value of pain and how to use it to make healthier choices.

A childhood where I understood why I had so much stomach pain and nausea. Where I knew about listening to my body and about working through normal muscle pain. Where I was taught how to nourish and support my body. Where I was taught to be grateful for my body and how it shows up for me each day?

Imagine if as a child we could start to put value on the experience of pain and how it can help and teach us.

As I got closer to graduating chiropractic school my husband and I were ready to start a family. When I got pregnant. I knew I wanted to learn as much as possible about the process my body would go through and how to support it naturally. I had been working on my pediatric and prenatal certification and was loving learning about the entire process.

This was a turning point for me, and I find it is for many women. It is one of the first times some of us as women think about the safety of everything being put in our bodies. Now that the choices affect more than just ourselves, there comes a new awareness with the desire to keep the baby safe. What we may have not had the motivation to change in our lifestyle for ourselves we are now motivated to do for the baby's safety.

My husband and I took Bradley natural childbirth classes which taught me more about fear, birth and pain. One of my most empowering learning experiences was going through natural childbirth. I faced and leaned into pain and overcame it.

Experiencing natural childbirth helped me realize how much my body can do and overcome on its own. This was an amazing experience for me to learn about pain and how it can be purposeful. I also gained an awareness how so much of our pain is caused by the mere anticipation, the fear of the unknown and the possible pain that could happen.

After the birth of my son, I was so grateful for the experience that I took classes, and I decided to become a certified Bradley Childbirth Teacher. I knew this was another part of my mission to share. I absolutely love being a mom and feel empowered to be able to use the research and resources I have gathered over the years to support my child's health.

My go to tools for motherhood included: Chiropractic care (checking the baby at birth and on), plant medicine using essential oils and clean healthy food and supplements.

When I was 36, I hit another turning point. My body was giving me new symptoms and course correcting clues. I woke up with a painful rash on my ribs near my belly button. I immediately knew what it was and that I needed to listen to what my body was saying.

This got my attention. 36-year-olds do not get shingles. It is very rare unless they are under high amounts of stress and their immune system is worn out. At this point in my life, I was a mother of a 6 and 3 year old and had been practicing Chiropractic for about 5 years. I was always pushing, as most working moms are, between running a small business and caring for the kids.

I pushed through the lack of sleep and low energy with coffee. My life had gotten out of balance and my body was letting me know. I went to a naturopath for direction. My tests showed I had adrenal fatigue, low immune function, and yes shingles. I was in shock. How did I let this happen? I get adjusted, I take supplements, I should know better.

The naturopath kindly helped me realize how out of balance my stress was. She suggested I incorporate more healing tools like yoga and acupuncture. I quickly made a course correction and added yoga, Heartmath meditation, acupuncture, immune supporting oils and supplements to my routine. I cut out all caffeine and went to bed as early as possible.

It took me a year to feel my energy levels return to normal, but they did. I could see the giant need for more tools for stress management. You can get adjusted, exercise, and eat well but if your stress is too high your health still suffers.

My life was so positively changed by adding yoga and acupuncture regularly to my life. I decided I had to learn more and add this to my mission to share with the world. Over the next few years, I took a Heartmath practitioner course, became a certified yoga instructor, and earned my acupuncture license.

I loved having these additional tools but still felt like something was missing. I could see how emotional stress was a sticking point not only for myself but for my patients and their ability to express health and heal fully. So, I continued to search and research.

As I turned 40, I began to become increasingly aware of more symptoms. I was unable to lose weight, started having frequent headaches, nausea and eczema on my face. The eczema on my face was new and got my attention.

I quickly made lifestyle adjustments to help but, everything I knew to try was not helping. I did some digging online and was recommended to try Remedy Testing by multiple chiropractors. My results gave me a roadmap of specific foods to cut out and some emotional stuck points for me to focus on.

When I was having the results of my test explained I had another breakthrough moment. The practitioner told me "Courtney you can make all these changes and cut out all these foods but if you don't address the emotions nothing will improve." She explained if your body perceives it is under a stress response, under an attack any food you put in your body during that time can also be associated as an irritant or threat.

Ok so here I was again being pointed to stress and emotions. I asked for her opinion on how to best do this. She recommended researching and reading more on quantum physics and frequency healing. I was aware of these topics but needed to dive deeper.

I followed all the recommendations consistently and for the first time cut out all dairy from my diet along with lots of other things that came up on my results. I have spent my life "guinea pigging" as I like to call it with diets, detoxes, supplements, therapies, techniques, protocols, gadgets and tools, searching for effective health enhancements. Making this strict diet change took effort but was nothing new to me and I was 100 percent committed. I knew this was another tool I had to share on my mission and studied to become a Remedy Health coach.

Results were slow at first but after a few months I started to see big changes. My eczema cleared up on my face and headaches and nausea were now rare. I started losing the stuck weight and feeling healthier and more energetic. I continued with the food elimination and journaling on the emotions presented on my test.

As suggested, I was also doing more research and that is how I came across Holographic Manipulation Therapy (HMT) and Dr. Gabe Roberts. As I read the way he explained and wrote about the connection between the nerve system, symptoms, emotions, and traumas I again felt that magnetized feeling. I knew immediately I had to learn everything I could from him and enrolled to study with him.

HMT has taught me an awareness of a higher level of connection between the brain and body and between consciousness and pain. When I am doing an HMT session I feel a greater ability to connect awareness between my body and my brain. With each practice I feel the connection is easier and getting stronger just like training a muscle to get stronger.

Imagine having this metaphorical plug that is dangling from the brain that is able to connect to the body, but it is dangling and not connected and not plugged into the body. HMT has taught me how to close the loop and plug that cord into my body for a full charge, connection, and awareness. When I practice now, I like to mentally visualize connecting and plugging in an imaginary awareness charging cord from my brain to my body.

HMT is able to bring a laser focus to where feelings are stored in the body and gives us the opportunity to recognize these feelings and to rewrite and replace uncomfortable or unwanted feelings. It is a tool like no other that brings a new level to healing and self-care. It is an amazing technique that we can learn to incorporate into our daily routines, one I know is part of my mission to share.

Below is a description a client gave about their first HMT session we did together.

"Before the HMT session, I was not aware of any connection between past experiences that were traumatic in nature, and my current pain and health issues. Dr. Courtney Davis started my session by asking me if I had a physical condition that I would like to have addressed as an area of focus. I chose my neck area. I had undergone a cervical fusion two years prior, and was currently having some numbness in my left hand, which was previously found to be connected to the cervical issues.

The process that Dr. Davis implemented, helped me to visualize an image of myself and to shrink that image down into the area of the cervical issues. With closer examination I was able to recognize the image as myself when I was a little girl at a time of emotional trauma. I clearly saw that the little girl had bangs. The bangs allowed me to determine the age of the little girl, which helped me to determine the incident that had occurred. I now understand that the incident may have started a cycle of feelings that became associated with and contributed to disease of the cervical area. This treatment with Dr. Davis helped me to expand my awareness about possible causes of health issues other than just physical experiences. "

One of the applications I am most excited about using HMT during is in supporting the Pregnancy and birth experience. Pregnancy is a wonderful time to implement the mind and body work of chiropractic, acupuncture and HMT. The increasing and changing demands on the structure and organ systems in the pregnant body get great benefit and support from wellness care.

There is this wonderful newfound courage that turns on in many pregnant women where they are seeking positive health changes and natural solutions.

Courage that they may not have had to make positive changes for just themselves but are now motivated with a new awareness now that their choices affect their baby as well. Suddenly there is a desire to clean up the diet, their environment and to have safe drugless solutions to protect the babies' development.

Unfortunately, it can also be a time of many emotions of fear and uncertainty. Women are often flooded with tales from others of their negative experiences with pregnancy and stories of others' birth trauma. This is a vital time for women to do work like HMT to mentally prepare for a positive pregnancy and birth experience.

I have seen much pain and fear presented in pregnancy due to an unknowing about the normal shifts and sensations that the body goes through in pregnancy and birth. Many times, we can be soothed with the mere understanding of what the pain sensation is telling us. When women know what is causing their pain and that it is often just normal shifting and changes happening and not harm happening the fear factor is removed and they have much relief in that knowledge alone.

In natural childbirth we are taught to relate pain to positive progress. As the pain and pressure sensation moves down the pelvis the birth of the baby comes nearer. The sensations of contractions intensifying means the contractions are more productive and creating more progress and the sooner the joy of the baby arriving will come.

What a wonderful time to prepare ourselves for the calling of motherhood by renewing our minds with a tool like HMT.

As I experience each of my future symptoms or pains, I will be ready and listening, looking to study and learn from each experience. I hope to continue to grow and be led to find more answers to the body's clues. I believe the answers are out there somewhere and some are just within ourselves needing to be uncovered.

As a young competitive gymnast Dr. Davis was often around injuries and early on became fascinated with the body and injury prevention and healing. She loves to research nutrition and tools to optimize health and wellbeing to utilize in practice. Dr. Davis is a native Tucsonan who graduated from the University of Arizona in 2002 with a Bachelor of Science in Biology and a minor in Chemistry. She received her doctorate in chiropractic in 2007 from Northwestern Health

Sciences University in Minneapolis, Minnesota. Dr. Davis is a member of the International Chiropractic Pediatric Association, has received certification in the Webster Technique, Pregnancy and Postpartum Corrective Exercise Specialist, Acupuncture, Yoga and Sound Therapy. Dr Davis is also a certified Softwave Technician and HOCATT Technician. Dr. Davis holds specialty certification in pediatrics and prenatal chiropractic.

Along with practicing Chiropractic Dr. Davis is a certified childbirth educator. She enjoys staying very active outdoors and spending free time gardening and hiking. Dr. Davis has been serving Tucson since 2008 with over 70,000 chiropractic adjustments.

Connect with me at
www.drcourtneyndavis.com
drcourtneydavis@gmail.com

Chapter Five
Finding my Voice
My Healing Journey after a Thyroid Cancer Diagnosis
Dr Booke Silberhorn DC

When you find the courage to use your voice, it has the power to positively inspire and change the lives of others. It's one of the special gifts you have to offer the world and is something to be cherished and championed, never hidden. ~Nicole O'Neill

"Brooke, it's what we thought. It is Thyroid Cancer." I will never forget where I was when I heard my doctor speak those words from the other end of the phone. That moment was life-altering. Those two words held a weight that many have crumbled under. Yet, I was prepared.

It had only been two weeks since I saw a Thyroid specialist, had an ultrasound, and was told a biopsy was recommended due to concern for Thyroid Cancer. To be honest, the possibility of cancer was almost worse than the actual diagnosis. In those two long weeks, I'd spent a lot of time crying, praying, talking with family and friends, and searching out natural healing methods.

It was also during that time I asked myself some hard questions like "What do I believe?" As a Doctor of Chiropractic, I tell my patients, "You are amazing. Your body is designed to self-correct, self-heal, and self-regulate. You are made to thrive!" I had to ask myself if I truly believed all the things I say about the body, health, healing, and function because it would dictate the steps I would take in the days, weeks, months, and years to come.

One of my business mentors, Shawn Dill, often says, "There is no one right way to do anything, but there is a right way for you." After taking time to pray and sit with my options, I determined that those beliefs were true for me and that the most authentic approach for me was to use natural healing methods. In the pages to follow, I will share highlights of my healing journey as well as the lessons I learned along the way and how I now use them to help others. I hope that it will help you find your way in your own journey to optimal health and thriving life!

Lesson 1: *Look in the mirror.*

Two years before I was diagnosed with Thyroid Cancer (almost to the day!), I found out I was pregnant with my youngest daughter, Ashlyn. It was an exciting time, but just a few weeks later, my boss (at the time) mentioned that my thyroid appeared to be enlarged. When my Thyroid labs were all within the normal range, I didn't think much of it and continued preparing for her birth.

Fast forward to when Ashlyn was about three months old, she began showing signs of Eczema. This then led me on a months-long quest to discover the source of her condition. I cut out wheat and dairy products from my diet, switched laundry detergent and cleaning products, and more. Her eczema would clear up for a brief time…only to return weeks later. It was very frustrating, yet I was convinced that I would find the cause!

During that entire time, my thyroid fluctuated in size. Once in a while, I would have someone ask me about it, but I did nothing until I saw a picture of myself from a family wedding. It was a wonderful picture of my husband and me. I looked great…but my thyroid was huge. That "look in the mirror" was what I needed to finally stop chasing my daughter's symptoms and start looking at my own. Hindsight is 20/20, but looking back it's now obvious that her symptoms reflected the inflammation and dis-ease (lack of ease leading to disease) in my body that I was just passing to her via breastmilk.

Lesson 2: *It's not bad genes…it is how they are expressing themselves. AKA: Preconception Health Matters.*

Many people, when they experience a health challenge like heart disease or cancer, tend to blame faulty genetics. They say things like "it runs in my family." The more we learn about human genetics and more specifically epigenetics, however, we are finding that this is not a path set in stone.

According to the CDC, Epigenetics is defined as the study of how your behaviors and environment can cause changes that affect the way your genes work. Making changes to your environment and behaviors, like your diet and exercise habits, can cause epigenetic changes to your gene expression, kind of like turning a light switch on or off.

Based on this information we can learn two things. First, we are not a victim of our genetics. We can make changes that can alter the trajectory of our personal health. Second, by making changes in our own lives, we can change the lives of future generations!

One of the reasons I so confidently stepped into the natural healing methods is because of the path forged by my friend and mentor Dr. Marcia Schaefer. Similar to my own journey, Dr. Marcia was diagnosed with Thyroid Cancer when her son was less than 4 months old. After having her thyroid removed, and then receiving additional diagnoses of metastases to her lungs and skin cancer, she returned to what she knew about natural healing and used Gerson therapy to restore her health and function.

When I was diagnosed, Dr. Marcia was one of the first people I knew to reach out to. What she told me reaffirmed the path I would take. She said, "My one regret is that I had my thyroid removed out of fear before I did my own research. I can't get that back."

As Dr. Marcia shared what she learned from her healing experience, she not only influenced my life but the lives of her practice members, as well as the patients and practice members of other chiropractors like myself. Her journey made her realize that trying to heal from cancer is often too little, too late. Her mission, like my own, became to use the principles of epigenetics to help create healthy humans by helping couples become healthy *before they conceive*.

Like I said in lesson 1, hindsight is 20/20. I wish I had understood this prior to conceiving both of my daughters. Preconception health, or Conscious Conception, is not just about getting pregnant. It is about expressing the best version of yourself prior to conception, physically, mentally, and emotionally, so you can pass along that genetic expression to your children and generations to come!

Lesson 3: *It doesn't matter what other people think. You pick your version of hard.*

There is no one right way to heal. But there is a right way for you. When I was researching different options for healing, I was introduced to a website called ChrisBeatCancer.com. Chris has an inspiring story of healing from Stage 3 Colon Cancer and also interviews people who have healed using natural methods. It was amazing how each person's journey was unique to them!

When you decide the best version of healing for you, know that you aren't going to please everyone. You will have well-meaning family, friends, and strangers who will think you are doing it wrong. You will also have people who support you and cheer you on. But neither of them matters. What matters most is the conviction you have in the path you are on, because healing can be hard work.

When I was about four months into my healing journey, I attended my 15-year High School reunion. For months I had been in my little bubble of support and encouragement, so I had no hesitation in sharing the approach I was taking to healing. I didn't think twice when asked by a former classmate how things were going. I said something to the effect of "It's going well. I feel great. I drink 10-13 cups of fresh veggie and fruit juice a day. And I do coffee enemas to detoxify the liver." This person (who, by the way, happens to be a medical professional) said, "Ew."

Now, I could have allowed her comments to derail me or make me question what I was doing. Instead, I learned from her comments. The opinions of others do not matter. I'll be totally honest, this is a lesson I'm still learning.

There are days I still worry about what other people think of me and the choices I make in life, health, and business. But at the end of the day…and the end of your life, your feelings about your journey are what matters most. Here I am writing about my healing journey almost 9 years later. Even though it was hard work at times, I must have done something that worked for me, because I'm still here!

Lesson 4: *Self-Care isn't Selfish (and it isn't sexy)*

If you've traveled anywhere by plane, you've heard the following safety instructions: "In the event of loss of cabin pressure, an oxygen mask will drop down in front of you. To start the flow of oxygen, pull the mask towards you. Place it firmly over your nose and mouth, secure the elastic band behind your head, and breathe normally. Although the bag does not inflate, oxygen is flowing to the mask. *If you are traveling with a child or someone who requires assistance, secure your mask first and then assist the other person.*"

As a wife, mom, small business owner, chiropractor, and nurturer by nature, I often used to put the needs of others ahead of my own. So, when I heard those "two words", I realized something needed to shift. If I didn't take care of myself, I wouldn't be around to care for the ones I love most. In my quest to figure out what was causing my daughter's eczema, I had lost sight of this important lesson: to take care of myself. I had to put myself first. I needed to put on my own oxygen mask.

For a while, I told myself that I needed to be a little selfish. I didn't feel bad about it, but as I've continued to work on myself over the years, I have learned it is just the opposite. Self-care isn't selfish. It is an act of love for yourself and others. Being your best self doesn't take away from others…it adds to their life experience!

Self-care also is not "sexy." It isn't necessarily pampering yourself with pedicures, facials, and massages (though those are great monthly options!). Self-care is doing the simple daily habits that support your body's natural healing rhythms. It is hydration, eating nutritious meals, getting rest, moving your body, breathwork and meditation, and getting checked by your chiropractor. It can also be taking your essential nutrient supplements, prepping veggies for juice, and the less-than-sexy coffee enemas!

My self-care has not always looked the same over the years. Exercise programs change. My morning routine changes with shifts in my energy, cycle, and business and family schedules. But one thing remains. I do it. I do it for myself, my family, and the people I care for.

Lesson 5: *Don't miss the forest for the trees.*

A couple of months into my healing journey, I got home from work and made dinner for my family. (I continued to do both of those things while also focusing on my personal healing.) After I got dinner on the table, we sat down and prayed for the meal. My family then began to eat, and I immediately got up from the table to start making my last round of juices for the day.

I had done this every day, day in and day out, for months. But this night was different. My family finished their dinner, and I was still making juice. As I stood in front of the juicer, I looked out the kitchen window at my family as they sat on the swings in our backyard…enjoying the summer evening. At that moment I realized that I had been so focused on one thing that I was missing out on the rest of my life!

It is so easy to get tunnel vision. Whether it is a new relationship, your business, or healing, many of us tend to throw ourselves into whatever is in front of us at the moment. But that means other things suffer… and that is not true health and wholeness in life!

Dorland's Medical Dictionary defines Health as "an optimal state of physical, mental, and social well-being, and not merely the absence of disease or infirmity." Completely missing out on my family's life while I focused on my healing…was not healthy! I chose to make some minor shifts after that day, and my whole life was better for it.

Lesson 6: *Stop looking for something to blame*

When I was first diagnosed, I nearly drove myself crazy trying to figure out what happened to lead me down this path. Was it my diet? Did I not eat healthy enough? Was it because I grew up in a small town in IA…surrounded by corn fields where pesticides were sprayed? Was it due to using a form of hormonal birth control for 3 years after my first daughter was born? Was my body somehow defective?

There are two pieces to this lesson. First, there is not one singular cause of dis-ease. This lesson was one that I'd learned long before Thyroid cancer, but sometimes you need a reminder of lessons learned long ago.

In Chiropractic we talk about the 3 T's: Thoughts (mental stress), Trauma (physical stress), and Toxins (chemical stress). Dis-ease in the body is due to the body's inability to adapt to the accumulation of stresses we are overwhelmed by in life. It's not just one thing…it is all of them!

The second piece to this lesson answers the question "Is my body broken or defective?" Disease and Dysfunction do not mean broken and defective. Symptoms are signals. They are signals from your body to make a change. It is your body's intelligent response to too much stress!

Lesson 7: *Our life experiences are not good or bad. They are two sides of the same coin.*

In 2015 my family and I moved from IL to FL where I then opened my chiropractic practice. Seeking to grow myself in order to grow my practice, led me down the next leg of my healing journey.

If you've ever looked back on different experiences and seasons of your life you may experience emotions of guilt, shame, pride, and resentment. Guilt over that friend you hurt in middle school. Shame over the choices you made. Pride about the people you've helped. Resentment toward the people you've been hurt by. Relationships that ended badly. Job loss. Divorce.

My mentor Dr. Alok Trivedi taught me that a new level of healing and wholeness comes when we see all of those experiences as just that. Experiences that are neither good nor bad. New levels of freedom came from finding the drawbacks of things I perceived to be good. (For example, success in business requires better organization, more time, and more money for marketing.)

Healing came from finding the benefits of the things I perceived to be bad. For example, the "bad" ending of my first marriage was the best beginning of the life I love today. If my first husband and I had not gotten divorced, I wouldn't have eventually moved to IL, met and married my husband Jason, given birth to my youngest daughter, or opened my practice in FL!

Lesson 8: *Live aligned to your Cyclical Design*

A few years ago I started seeing a pattern. Every month I would have a day where I felt like a failure in life and business, nothing was working, and I should just give up. I observed this for several months before I finally asked a group of fellow female chiropractors if they had ever experienced something similar.

One doctor suggested I read the book *Do Less* by Kate Northrup. I got it on Audible and listened to it 3 times in just over a week! That then led me to take a deep dive into the world of women's cycles, cycle syncing, and cyclical living.

(Guys…don't stop reading here…if you have any women in your life at all, this lesson will help you in your relationship too!)

I never once associated the "anxious" feelings I was having each month with my menstrual cycle. I was at a place in my life as a woman where my period was healthy, and it came and went without incident.
Symptom-free periods were not always a way of life for me.

In my teens and early twenties, I would get horrible headaches and cramps with my period. After I gave birth to my oldest daughter, the cramps stopped, but the headaches became full-blown migraines. As a chiropractor, I get adjusted regularly, but no adjustment would touch these. Thankfully, after I started juicing, gently detoxing my body, and supporting better function in my body, the migraines gradually went away!

When I read *Do Less*, and later other books about Cyclical Living, how I did life and business changed for the better. Even though I learned about the menstrual cycle in high school, college, and chiropractic college, it was never presented in this way! Like the phases of the moon and the seasons in nature, the phases of my cycle have different hormonal shifts, nutritional needs, and energy levels. Now I eat, exercise, rest, and even market my business in alignment with my cyclical design and I teach women to do the same!

Lesson 9: *Labs can Lie and your vibration is everything!*

Before I was diagnosed with Thyroid Cancer, my blood labs were normal. A couple of years later, my weight suddenly ballooned and my energy dipped, but my labs were all normal. In my case…and the case of many others, blood labs did not give a true reflection of what was going on in my body.

It wasn't until I learned about Remedy Testing, a bioenergy test, that I was able to dig deeper into the specific stresses causing dis-ease in my body. If you have health challenges but are struggling to find answers, this is one of the best ways I've found to do just that! Bioenergetic, or quantum, hair analysis uses vibrational frequencies to test your hair tissue for organ function, emotional stress patterns, nutritional and hormone imbalances, food and environmental sensitivities, toxin exposures, and more!

If you've ever played with tuning forks, you will find that two tuning forks of the same vibrational frequency will resonate with each other. Two tuning forks of different frequencies will not. Similarly, Bioenergy Testing works by testing known vibrational frequencies of 1000s of things in our body and environment and seeing if our hair tissue resonates with the same frequency. Every cell in your body vibrates, and your nervous system communicates via vibration, so you are literally a walking talking tuning fork!

What do you resonate with? Is it the frequencies of grief and hatred, or love and joy? Are you resonating with the frequencies of bacteria, parasites, and viruses? Are you eating foods that your body does not resonate with, therefore causing inflammation and dysfunction? By learning the sources of stress causing dysfunction in my body, I have been able to continually listen to my body, make changes, and raise my vibration. A wonderful byproduct of doing this testing and making changes, I've experienced better health and function than when I was in my 20s!

Lesson 10: *Creating Coherence*

I've been getting adjusted by chiropractors since I was about 6 years old. Growing up, we went to the chiropractor when we were hurt or sick, or if there was a snowstorm and "normal" people would cancel their appointments. My dad would call to see if there were openings, load us all up, and make the snowy 22-mile drive to get adjusted!

Chiropractic has been and will always be part of my health habits, but a few years ago, I began wanting to see even greater changes in myself and my practice members than what I was seeing and experiencing. I thought about a technique I was exposed to as a student and experienced great results, so I decided to jump in and learn it, and also receive it for myself.

I know everyone is different, so what works best for me may not work great for you. But what I found is that for years, I would get adjusted 2-3 times per week, and still struggle with the same physical challenges. Once I started getting adjusted using Network Spinal Technique, my nervous system function started to improve. Network Spinal, which was developed by Donald Epstein, DC, focuses less on moving a vertebra, and more on the tone and tension of the spine and spinal cord. This allows for greater coherence within the nervous system, and for natural healing waves to move through the body.

I like to say that by using Network Spinal in my life and my practice, I focus on getting more out of life instead of less of a symptom.

Lesson 11: *I don't respond to stress with Fight or Flight*

As I continue to learn as much as I can about the nervous system, one of the best things I've learned in recent years as a practitioner and as a person is the Polyvagal Theory. Polyvagal Theory suggests that our autonomic nervous system responds to stress in different ways depending on what branch is stimulated or dominant. You've probably heard of the Fight or Flight response. That is the response of our Sympathetic Nervous System (what I call our "gas pedal") in a state of stress. This is a response to stress more typically seen in men.

The dorsal branch of our Parasympathetic Nervous System (what I like to call our "brake pedal") is commonly associated with how it responds in a state of ease: rest, healing, and digestion. In stress, it is the freeze or "deer in the headlights" response. I don't know about you, but I've definitely been there.

Polyvagal theory furthers our understanding and describes how the ventral branch of the Parasympathetic Nervous System, our "Social Vagus," responds to stress by either fawning (saying yes when you really want to say no) or fitting in (blending/merging with others and not standing out). Because our desire is to be part of a tribe or a family, the female response to stress is typically one of these two. Wow. When I first heard this, I realized how many times in my life I diminished myself and tried to fit in instead of standing out and using my voice, all because I was in such a high state of stress.

Lesson 12: *Mental/Emotional Trauma is the greatest cause of dis-ease and dysfunction*

As I discussed in Lesson 5, there are three types of stress, but the one thing I've observed in practice (and in my own life) is that mental/emotional stress or trauma is the greatest source of dis-ease in the body. You can eat all organic, exercise regularly, take all the best supplements, and still be incredibly unhealthy.

I've done a lot of work on my mindset over the years, especially after I learned that there are emotional stress patterns that relate to dysfunction in different parts of the body. In my personal situation, Thyroid/Throat challenges often relate to not "speaking your truth" or using your voice.

The more I have reflected on my past, I've seen a recurring pattern of staying silent to the point of holding tension in my throat so as not to rock the boat or risk someone not liking me. No wonder I was diagnosed with Thyroid Cancer. I was storing trauma after trauma in my throat!

Here is the fantastic thing. As I have done mindset work, vibrational healing, and psychosomatic healing methods like Holographic Manipulation Therapy (HMT), I will see and feel physical changes to the appearance and feel of my thyroid!

Lesson 13: *I don't remember.*

As I have done the deeper mental/emotional healing work, I have long felt that there was something I was missing. Initially, I worked on more recent experiences including work frustrations, the end of my first marriage, and the abuse I experienced in that relationship. Then experiences in high school and middle school. A lot of healing came from processing those things, but I still felt like there was something more.

Eventually, I traced back to a series of several root experiences that happened around ages 5-6. I had a teacher deny me going to the bathroom, causing me to pee my pants. I had a Sunday school teacher spank me. I had a doctor not believe me when I broke my arm. (He went so far as to grab my arm and jerked it back and forth to prove his point, absolutely forcing me into a freeze response.) All of these root experiences are linked to not feeling heard. Not being able to use my voice.

Yet, I felt there was more. Something earlier. Something I just didn't remember. Then I was introduced to Holographic Manipulation Therapy and Psychosomatic Medicine.

My first introduction was a one-day workshop Dr. Gabe Roberts taught. As he walked us through some of the methods, I began to feel lighter, and freer. At the end of the day, Dr. Gabe asked for a volunteer to go through a full regression, and I volunteered. I wanted it all!

In that regression, I went back to the moment of my birth. My mom had shared stories with me about how the Doctor had to use forceps to turn my head so I wouldn't be born with a broken nose, but during the regression, I felt all the fear I felt even before I was actually born! To be able to reframe that root experience was definitely life-altering!

Lesson 14: *Finding my voice. AKA Hear me Roar!*

2022 was a big year of deep healing work for me. It was finally time. I was finally ready to put together every lesson that I'd learned and to stand up and be heard.

I went through a period in May where I felt energetically like I was in a cocoon. I struggled to do much because I felt "off", but I knew I was just in the "in between." My friend/mentor/coach Mel Krug described it as energetically being like a trapeze artist who has let go of one bar…but has not yet grabbed hold of the other. I was preparing for something big, just like a caterpillar being transformed into a butterfly.

And then I went to two healing immersions in the fall. At the first healing immersion, I had so many breakthroughs, it is hard to fully describe what I experienced. But on the last (optional) day of the event, Dr. Donald Epstein said some things that cut to my heart. He said many people don't survive big health challenges (like cancer) because they don't get angry.

Anger requires energy…and so does healing! So expressing anger and vocalizing it, instead of holding it in, helps with healing. Wow. Never once do I recall expressing emotion like that. I just prayed., trusted God, and trusted my body. But I also held stuff in.

I took the opportunity that day to share my takeaways, and I shared my big fear. I worried that if I shared my healing journey and all that I've learned, but then cancer comes back… people would be upset with me. My biggest fear was what other people think. So Dr. Donny told me, "Brooke, I'm going to ask you to do something for me. (Cue the sound guy playing a clip of a roaring lion.) I want you to stand in front of this crowd of people, and I want you to ROAR."

At that moment I had two options. Worry what other people would think of me. I mean. Roar like a lion? In a hotel conference room? In front of over 100 people? That's weird! Or, I could use my voice.

So, I leaned forward and brought up a low rumble from deep within my belly and let out a long, loud ROAR. I did it twice. I allowed my voice to be heard. I allowed my body to feel those deep healing vibrations through every cell, so I would remember. I remember that I am strong. I am powerful. I have a message that is crying to be heard. My message brings hope and healing to others…and myself.

And you do too.

Dr. Brooke Silberhorn has been a Doctor of Chiropractic since 2007. In 2015, she opened Thrive Chiropractic and Wellness in Ocala, FL. Her mission is to help women be empowered in their health and life, so they and their families can thrive!

In addition to providing gentle chiropractic care for the whole family, Dr. Brooke offers in-person and online wellness consultations to discuss how she can serve you best. Other services include Preconception/ Fertility Health programs, Women's Health/Life Coaching, Remedy Testing, Intuitive Life Coaching, and Holographic Manipulation Therapy. For more information and to schedule a complimentary consultation, Dr. Brooke's website is *thrivewithchiro.com*

Chapter Six

Evolution is an inside job; untangling what doesn't belong to discover true essence within
By: Nina Hermann

Everything changes when you start to emit your own frequency rather than absorbing the frequencies around you, when you start imprinting your intent on the universe rather than receiving an imprint from existence.

– Barbara Marciniak

I spent hundreds of thousands of dollars between health devices, gadgets, supplements, treatments, retreats, seminars, programs, licenses, and certifications. Everything I did only disguised or masked the situation without actually healing me, causing the process to be prolonged. I was seeking external help and I discovered that the answer is the innate intelligence within me that was there the entire time.

My hope is for others to take a more direct route to living fully and embracing their true essence than I did. My 15 year long and painful healing journey led me to this exact moment to know and share that I am powerful beyond measure when I turn within. I am no different than anyone else. My journey was far longer than it needed to be, but I refused to believe that fact until I could no longer refuse its truth.

Nature doesn't do anything that doesn't make sense and we are no different. However, we are far more complex thinking beings who complicate matters with our thinking brain that gives into the programming and beliefs that are laid upon us. As I began to shed the outdated beliefs and programing and recognize the Divine within, my life began to change dramatically.

Pain and symptoms are an indicator that something is wrong. Sadly, we jump in and immediately try to resolve the symptoms, taking over-the-counter medications or seeking assistance from a doctor or other health professional, who wants to help, but symptom management is merely masking and putting a band-aid on the real problem. Sadly, the more I learn, it is not just that we are masking, but we aren't actually healing the body and even worse we are actually interrupting and prolonging the healing process. Our bodies know exactly what to do if we don't interrupt. We just have to understand what is going on in our bodies and support the process.

I believe there are no coincidences. People come in and out of our lives for a reason, a season, a lesson, or a lifetime. The most profound healing I've discovered is German New Medicine, also known as Germanic New Medicine and Germanic Heilkunde, seen abbreviated as GNM, GH or GHk.

In 2019, I was scheduled to attend an event in Atlanta. I never share a room with someone unless I'm going with people I know and we book together. This particular event used an app for the attendees to be able to connect prior to the event. I had never seen such connection and coordination happening, it was really amazing. I noticed several were connecting with each other to share a hotel room at the event. I thought, well, why not. I posted and received responses right away.

The first was debating on her situation and with the second, Andi Locke Mears, I felt an energetic connection right off the bat. We decided to have a phone call to determine if we would be compatible. I asked her what she did and she told me that she was a German New Medicine consultant and instructor and she facilitated the GNM USA group.

I immediately questioned what it was. As Andi begins to explain, I asked, "What is the doctor's name?", and she replies "Dr. Ryke Hamer". I then went to my book shelf, pulled off a book and saw that the section that I remembered was written by Dr. Hamer. I had heard of his work.

In 2014, I was separated from my now ex-husband and he was diagnosed with cancer. I had been studying alternative health methods for some time at that point and had attended numerous healing workshops. I had come across this book called, *Cancer Report* at one of them, which was a compilation of different authors on healing cancer. Dr. Hamer's section rang loud and clear to me and I immediately went to my husband at the time and had him come over.

We sat on our back lanai overlooking the lagoon that our home backed up to and I told him about what I had learned and that he could heal it, we could heal.

It was very clear to me that the trauma we had just been through and was outlined so very clearly by Dr. Hamer's words was what caused his type of cancer. He wasn't interested. He was good. I was disappointed but recognized it was his journey and there was nothing I could do about it.

Fast forward to what I know today in 2023 after taking a course on the biology of men from a Germanic New Medicine perspective. I am clear that the way I approached him triggered his masculinity ending with him saying he didn't need help. I didn't know anyone else with cancer at the time, and I put the book back on the shelf. The information stuck with me, however, I wish I had known at the time, it wasn't limited to cancer.

Back in 2019 and now in Atlanta with my conference with Andi, she began to share more details of Dr. Hamer's work. It applied to all healing—not just cancer—by looking at the body biologically, as nature intended. At the time, I was dealing with Interstitial Cystitis (IC) and the best way I can describe it is that it's like ulcers on the bladder. I also had I don't know how many UTIs throughout my life, and had been on countless anti-biotics. I was in the midst of an IC flare, and I had been dealing with it for nearly two years with varying levels of intensity.

She was describing a bank robbery and how there are several people involved, but each will view this trauma from a different perspective. Someone may view as his or her territory and how dare this robber do this to my territory or my bank. This person would then have UTI/bladder issues with their conflict and resolution.

I thought about it, and I looked at her and told her my issues and said, "I'm not territorial, this doesn't make sense to me." Oh, but then it hit. I am so controlling and territorial about certain things. I spent the next week meditating and contemplating what I just learned. I meditated on the idea of what's mine is yours and what's yours is mine.

I had read the book, *The Science of Getting Rich* by Wallace Wattles and I knew and believed that resources are unlimited, there is enough to go around and we are supported by the Divine. I will always have everything I need and will always be taken care of. I spent the time every day, repeating, meditating, noticing and remembering where those statements were true.

I also sat in gratitude for the people that were in my life or had been in my life, thanking them for the contribution and lessons they helped teach me. I believe and understand that not everyone is meant to stay a lifetime in our lives. I can grieve their loss when it's time for their departure, and can be grateful for all the time I had with them. Within a week of focusing and spending time every day going over what I just shared, the flare subsided completely. I did not have another UTI or Interstitial

Cystitis flare again for two years. I still have not had another UTI since then.

In 2021, my landlord—after she promised to allow me to continue to rent her house on Anna Maria Island through 2022—decided she had to take advantage of the current real estate market and she needed to sell, which meant, I had to move out. I didn't know where I was going to go. The rental market had doubled, if not tripled in some areas, especially on the Island. I didn't want to be forced to buy a place in that market in a short amount of time. I didn't know where I wanted to be located either.

And you could probably guess, the Interstitial Cystitis reared its ugly head. Only this time, I was equipped with knowledge and I knew exactly what was going on. I spent the next week in the same manner, focusing on the fact that I know everything will work out, this was meant to happen and it was time for me to move on.

Sure enough, within a week, it was gone, and to date, hasn't returned.

Oh what a glorious world we would live in if we were all equipped with the knowledge of Germanic Heilkunde and could recognize and heal so quickly. This is my vision.

So how does GNM work? It was founded by Dr. Hamer, whose son was shot while on vacation in 1978 and died four months later. The doctor and his wife were both diagnosed with cancer. Dr. Hamer questioned whether or not it was a coincidence or if the trauma they went through caused the cancer. He spent the rest of his life and studied over 40,000 cases and heard even more than 60,000 cases. In 100% of them, there was a shock, trauma or conflict in that person's life prior to their diagnosis.

How did he study these cases? When we experience the shocking, isolating event, based on how our psyche perceives the conflict, there will be a lesion in the brain tied to that conflict and an area of the body impacted. Those with the same perception/same conflict perceived by the psyche had the lesion in the same area of the brain and the same area of the body impacted. The lesion can be detected in a CT scan of the brain. Dr. Hamer did CT scans for each person and interviewed the individual as to what was going on in that person's life and what their symptoms were.

It wasn't just the trauma, it was the perception of the person's psyche that determined how the body would respond. Our body is brilliant and it is always trying to keep us safe. Our bodies respond in one of three ways: cell loss / necrosis, cell growth /proliferation or loss of function (organ/nerve). It is going to do what it perceives as necessary in order to help us through the threat we are experiencing.

Think in biologic terms, what would happen in nature. When we resolve the conflict and the psyche perceives us safe, the body then brings us back to homeostasis. Where we had cell loss, we now have cell growth/replenishment. Where we had cell growth, we now have cell breakdown. Where we lost function, we now regain.

Depending on the germ layer of the body, you can determine what would be happening in the body if conflict is active or if in the post conflict stage. We can also incur what is referred to as a hanging healing. This is where we resolve the conflict, but then are triggered again or have a recurrence of the trauma/conflict and the body goes back and forth between the conflict active and conflict resolution stages.

Additionally, our subconscious is always trying to keep us safe and is taking in 2.3 million bits of information through our senses at any point in time. When we experience the conflict, our subconscious is taking in information through the senses and then uses that information in the future to alert us of the threat. This is called a tract. For instance, you are eating a peanut butter cookie when you receive unexpected news of a close family member's passing. Now, when you have peanut butter, you may have a reaction to it as your body's way of alerting you of a threat, given what you experienced the last time you ate peanut butter.

The beauty is that we can heal and resolve with conscious intention and desire by understanding how our body is trying to keep us safe. When we know what our body is doing, we can then support it while it does its thing and be in gratitude for its ability to keep us safe and protect us. Then we don't need to run to the doctor to interrupt the healing process.

Now, it does take effort on our part to understand, to look at things as they are and adjust our perception. It takes forgiveness, time and acceptance. Depending on how long the conflict active stage goes will play a factor in how long it takes the body in the post conflict active stage to heal.

There are other factors such as how healthy you are and what bacteria, fungi, virus, even fungi/candida and parasites you have in the body, as those microbes are needed in the cell loss and cell replenishment phases. Yes,our bodies need them! When we need them to help us through a conflict or heal from one, they will become active. When they are not needed, they go dormant or automatically remove themselves from your body. When you need them, your body will create an environment that attracts them into your body. There are more efficient and less efficient ways for the cell breakdown and replenishment, it just depends on what is within your body at the time of the conflict that your body can use.

Dr. Hamer mapped out symptoms and conflicts. The amount of information available from his dedication and life's work is beyond reproach. One can take a look at the symptoms they are dealing with and then look up the conflict. It sounds simple, and while it is, it is also very complicated. However, the direction, guidance and explanation is available to us to use as we work through to resolve the conflict.

My challenge with GNM and why it was not a top priority for me even though I saw miraculous healing from it stemmed from a couple of issues. First, in acute situations, it is easy to see what the conflict is and resolve. However, for chronic situations, it is not easy to remember when the symptoms started and what was going on in life prior to the symptoms. Second, it is a paradigm shift for healing and everything we've been taught thus far, so it's a far stretch for many to absorb. It's so simple at the core…how could it be so easy to heal. And some aren't willing to take responsibility and do what is necessary to heal themselves.

Over the last year to 18 months, it has been undeniable and continues to come up in situations all around me that it is so obvious what is needed to help someone heal that I can no longer sit by and watch others suffer trying to manage under the old paradigm of germ theory.

It was recently made available for me to have a CT scan of my brain and a professional — who trained with Dr Hamer — then read it and reviewed the results with me and my mentor. He identified numerous conflicts and they all made so much sense! I am still wrapping my head around and game planning how to resolve these. One of which was resolved the evening of the review.

While in our discussion of my CT scan, he mentioned that something happened about 6 months prior. I was going through everything I could possibly think of that happened in September of 2022. I couldn't come up with anything meaningful. Then that evening I was on a phone call with a friend, telling her about my review. It then hit me.

At the time I was living in a 5th wheel, travel trailer, but I did not have a truck to haul it. My intention was to purchase and then travel the nation, since I can work from anywhere and host retreats at various locations around the United States. I thought I could do it on my own, that I didn't need anyone to help me.

And then, I lived in it for a couple weeks, I watched the experienced professional deliver and park it, and I very quickly realized even if I could, it wasn't something I wanted to do by myself. I hadn't purchased a truck because the market for trucks was tough at the time. I also realized, I'm not a truck girl and didn't want to have to drive a dually around everywhere and have to park it.

So, in September of 2022, I'm in Bradenton, Florida and Hurricane Ian appears on the weather map. I have lived in Florida off and on since 1998 and I had been through the hoopla far too many times. It didn't faze me and I didn't plan for it. I don't watch TV or the news.

While on a group coaching call on a Tuesday morning, before the Hurricane was to hit land the following day. I listened and watched RV after RV (including travel trailers) vacate the RV park. I got multiple texts asking me what I was going to do and that I was under a forced evacuation. I grabbed my phone and looked up the NOAA website and pulled up the projected track. I was in the direct line of this hurricane.

The shock hit me hard. I had just picked up my brand new eight week old puppy Gracie the night before. I had no truck to haul my 5th wheel or a place to go to get it out of harm's way. When the coaching call was over, I just sat and cried, so angry at myself. How could I put myself in this position?

I could potentially lose my home. I had no idea if I have hurricane coverage on my insurance policy. I have no one to help me move it. What was I thinking? I felt isolated and all alone.

I did eventually get myself together, forced to do so since the county turned the water off. I put some personal items in the car and loaded my scared little Miss Gracie up to go stay with family. I put a mask on and enjoyed the time with my family.

The hurricane did end up turning in sooner than projected and hit further south. While we experienced some of the impact of the hurricane, we did not take a direct hit. Thankfully, I had zero damage to my unit, other than a fried electrical box at the park that left me without electricity for days, but I was fine, my belongings safe. My ego though, had not recovered.

I tell my friend about the incident, which she was familiar with as we have a mastermind call every week with another amazing woman. I'm in tears over the realization of the conflict. I had been in the car where I was dropping off a friend at her hotel during the call. After she got out and went to her hotel, I headed to the grocery store before heading home. By the time I got to the grocery store, I was in bad shape. I could barely see out of my right eye, it had become swollen. The head pain was excruciating. I could hardly function. I grabbed a couple items and headed home.

I was supposed to fly to Europe two days later. I had to postpone. I was horizontal with ice pack over my head. Healing happens in a liquid environment. When we resolve a conflict, and the body brings us back to homeostasis, whether the body is breaking down or replenishing, it brings in the microbes via liquid. The lesion in the brain also has to be repaired, which causes swelling and headaches. That was the second time I had witnessed healing take place so quickly. Both times within an hour of identifying/resolving a conflict.

Additionally, the professional who reviewed my CT scan told me that if we had identified correctly another conflict that we discussed, while on my trip to Europe, I would experience light bronchitis symptoms. I had completely forgotten about it, but it was in my notes. The Wim Hof expedition I was attending in Europe started Sunday night. Thursday morning I woke up sick.

I was going through my head what had happened the day before, which was a lot. I had done something I didn't think I could do. This Florida girl climbed Mount Śnieżka in shorts and a sports bra. We were later told that at the top the temperature with wind chill was -40 degrees. I did it. I thought I had resolved something by doing it. Then after returning, I was reading through my notes and noticed the comment. Oh My Goodness.

I am floored, beyond words of Dr. Hamer's brilliance and heart to serve. It saddens me to no end that this information has been suppressed for so long. There is not a significant financial gain when people can heal themselves. It is time, it is so time for this information to be in the light, for all to know, understand and apply!

I have been in search of methods and modalities to assist in chronic cases when there seems to be no correlation to a conflict, or one that can't be remembered. In some cases, that is a loss of function by the psyche to protect from remembering such a trauma. There is really no 100% clear and quick answer for everyone in all circumstances. However, through my own healing journey and how I came to know Dr. Tiffany Roberts and Dr. Gabe Roberts, I have learned how far superior Holographic Manipulation is to anything else I've experienced or witnessed. Additionally, breathwork of various types, but especially Emotional Energetic Release Therapy, has also been incredibly powerful and profound. The two combined with consistency were instrumental in my healing journey.

I started with the end result up front. As I was writing my healing journey, it repeatedly showed me the underworking's of GNM and felt that I needed to provide the basis up front.

THE HISTORY OF MY HEALING JOURNEY:

Prior to having the knowledge I have now with the help of the CT scan of my brain, here is the healing journey that led me on my path and what I could reflect as to what I was healing within myself.

My healing journey began in 2008 when I ended my term of service in the Army due to pain. I had pain in my neck, constant headaches, hip pain, and general body aches throughout most of my body, my hands and my feet. The Army's answer was medication, and I took a muscle relaxer, pain medication, and an anti-inflammatory every day and often multiple times a day. I did that for over four and a half years.

I knew there had to be a better answer and I started searching for answers then. However, looking back my true journey started New Year's Eve of 2013, when I held a ceremony for myself to officially divorce organized religion at the beach at sunset. I was then separated from the man who is now my ex-husband and there's nothing like a major life event such as a pending divorce to propel you into healing. And although I didn't intend for the ceremony to be such a big event in my life, my intention was to go to the beach and hold a ceremony at sunset letting go of everything that had happened in 2013, which was a lot in my personal life and within my family.

When I pulled up to park at the beach a song came on the radio that I hadn't heard before, "Say Something" (...I'm Giving Up On You) by A Great Big World. I realized I had given all my control and power over to my husband to love me and accept me for me and he had given it back. He couldn't take on that responsibility any longer and I realized I had given up on myself too, though long before that.

Now what? As I started to reflect in the few minutes I had before walking onto the beach, it was evident and so clear in my mind, I needed to let go of organized religion and the hypocrisy. I'm talking about the hypocrisy within myself first and foremost.

I walked out onto the sand, found shells that caught my attention and gathered them up. One by one, I identified what I was ready to let go of and I stated it to the shell and then threw the shell as far as I could and then watched the waves crash over it, washing it away. Mother Earth cleansed and made new.

I attached organized religion to the biggest shell I could find. As I threw it out, I wept, I sobbed. So much of my life I let go of in that instant and for a moment felt empty, but quickly realized it was the closest to me I had ever felt. Raw, open, vulnerable, yet I felt so supported, nurtured and held by Mother Earth and the Divine.

I sat down and watched as the sun set and continued to weep. I was grateful for all that had happened in my life, for closure, and for new beginnings. And even though I was sad too, I had never before felt so much hope for healing, for growth, and for truth to emerge. While that was one major step, it was only the beginning, as I started discovering who I am, what I believe, and why I am here.

My intention to heal was to be able to fully live. I spent far too much time not feeling alive, such that I didn't even want to live. My one word resolution for several years was "Alive". I just wanted to feel alive. I often had zero energy and was in constant pain, lacked hope and any kind of motivation. I was sad, lonely, felt isolated and in a daze. If it wasn't for my incredible parents, I'm certain I wouldn't be here.

When I think of my childhood, the first picture that would pop into my mind was a little girl with her bottom lip stuck out, sad, lonely, and afraid. I had the most amazing parents and a childhood that many would dream of having — yet on the inside — I was struggling, and always felt something was wrong with me but didn't know how to process or express it. I can remember times when neighborhood kids would come to play and they would be with my siblings on the swing set outside, and I would be inside, separate and alone and sad.

Given this amazing life I had, I've been asked, what I had to heal from since I didn't look sick and appeared to have everything one could wish for. In adulthood, the shame and guilt of needing healing given my experience compared to others haunted me and further confirmed the belief that something is wrong with me.

Despite ending my term of service because of pain, I never filed for disability even though my records were the size of a paper ream. Friends have continued to question me and borderline harass me (truly out of care and compassion) for not filing. I felt guilt over the thought of doing so and didn't need any additional concrete evidence that "something is wrong with me".

Pondering upon the question I believe I am healing from three experiences. The first of which I didn't understand until I was in my 30s and understood the impact of a mother's emotions on a baby in the womb. My grandmother committed suicide while my mother was pregnant with me. I was named after her, though, my parents couldn't bear to call me by her name, Nina, so they used my middle name, Lorene.

Side story. I started college at a junior college in Kansas City. My parents had purchased a condo across the street from the school and I worked at a local bank. I thought I had it all together. I was on my own, making money, going to college, and having fun, going out with my co-workers. I lived with my brother's girlfriend and my brother lived nearby.

The summer after my freshman year, my family and my brother moved to Florida and his girlfriend moved back home. I was all alone, but I wanted to prove that I was good – I didn't need help anymore – I had everything under control. Unfortunately, it wasn't long before I fell back into a sad place, and felt helpless.

Couple months later, I had mononucleosis. Learning German New Medicine, it is no wonder, I was experiencing a powerless conflict and/or a self-esteem conflict and potentially both. I was in an advanced Spanish course and I was failing miserably. My mother had always helped me in school and now I was on my own.

Once sick, my parents flew me down to Florida to take care of me, and when I arrived to Florida it was 80 degrees. I realized I had made a huge mistake not moving with my family and I transferred to the University of Tampa within two months. After the isolated, lonely experience back in Kansas, I was desperate for change. I made a decision when I moved, that I was no longer going to be that sad, lonely girl anymore.

At the same time, without thinking of it, I started to go by first name, Nina after going by my middle name Lorene, my entire life to that point. I didn't intentionally set out to do that, but I just got tired of correcting everyone, as my RAs in the college dorm had put Nina on my door and all my professors were addressing me as Nina. So I went with it.

I can look back now and see how consciously and unconsciously, my identity shifted as I started going by Nina. Who knew my name held such vibration and would change my identity along with it. My family to this day still calls me by my middle name, Lorene, unless referring to me as Aunt Nina for all my nieces and nephews.

The second experience, I have an audio processing delay. My brain doesn't process sound in normal ways. People think I have a hearing issue, as I often have to ask for something that was said to be repeated. I don't have a hearing issue, but it takes time for my brain to process the sound to determine what was said and sometimes, depending on the tone, it can't process at all.

As a diagnosis, it was determined that I had non-phonemic awareness, a form of dyslexia. I was slow in learning how to read and pronunciation was difficult. I was pulled out for remedial classes almost all of my school age years.

I was made fun of and bullied for this and how I pronounced words. As a result, I just shut up and didn't speak. When I did speak, I would be slow to respond, as I had to find words that I knew how to pronounce, to say what I wanted. Once again, the belief, something is wrong with me was confirmed. This no doubt contributed to a Self-Devaluation Conflict that I feel has been a hanging healing, for a significant part of my life. The lack of self-expression took its toll as well.

The third experience, I grew up in a fairly strict religious home. My parents are amazing, and they weren't raised that way, but they had become born again Christians before I was born. In my opinion, they were merely trying to abide by the standards they were learning and thought they needed to uphold. I never felt that I fit in or belonged, nor did I ever feel I could meet the standards and rules. I always felt judged and like I was never enough.

On the flip side, I also never felt I fit in with my secular school friends, which was frowned upon anyway. I was never bad enough or cool enough to fit in with them either. Therefore, again, the feeling that something is wrong with me was reinforced, and I isolated myself. I believe this was the beginning of an identity conflict, though still pinpointing a particular event, decision that contributed.

I will say the fourth and infinite items to heal from stemmed from overcoming (or rebelling) all the journeys taken while operating under beliefs and programming from the previous three experiences. Examples include proving myself and others wrong, etc. Some I will touch on and others I'm still working through.

I will at times have ups and downs. But as I described to a friend recently, I feel like the historical stock market, where I do have dips, but I soar higher after each dip, always rising over time. I am always trying to improve. However, I am in no shape even remotely experiencing the degree of pain, sadness, isolation, and fatigue I had felt for so long.

BACKGROUND LEADING UP TO 2008 AND HOW MY CAREER PATH EVOLVED:

In college I decided to do the ROTC program, which provided me a scholarship and a guaranteed job after college. I saw it as a way to force me outside of my comfort zone too. Following graduation and commissioning, I entered the United States Army as a second lieutenant in the Finance Corps.

Talk about a fish out of water but I managed to put a mask on, put a uniform on and show up every day. As the years went by the stress of being in uniform, doing something that I wasn't always aligned with, of always wondering if I was doing everything right, of always trying to fit in and not make any waves, and the stress of not expressing myself, took its toll on my mind and body.

As I mentioned before, due to the pain in my body, I was on three different medications daily. I had also been diagnosed with ADHD and was on prescription medication for that as well. I knew my body was toxic and the reality of it was, it was only taking the edge off my pain. I was suffering. I was struggling. I felt alone. I felt isolated and quite frankly I didn't want to be alive.

On November 2, 2007, I was driving from Ft. Bragg, NC to Asheville, NC for an art safari in Weaverville. I had to pull over and buy a notebook as an idea for a healing retreat center was brought to light. I had no idea of what healing could be other than doctors, hospitals and medication.

When I got out of the army the following year, my intent was to open a healing retreat center. The idea was no doubt something that was too big and I couldn't imagine starting something like that with no experience. When I got out of the Army, it was also 2008, and at that time, our economy and the market collapsed. I knew it wasn't a time for me to start a business.

I was still searching for what could help my pain. My mother had been Rolfed while I was in junior high school, and it had essentially cured her of pain that she had her entire life. She kept requesting that I go be Rolfed, but I remembered stories from my brother, who was being Rolfed at the same time as my mother, of this woman's elbow going up his nose.

My brother exaggerates, but he would talk of the excruciating pain often. I thought to myself, I'm just not that desperate…until I was. I was offered a job out of the blue to work for a Defense Contractor in Alaska. When I moved to Alaska, the very first day that I'm there, I was searching for a place to live with a realtor. We come to a stop light; I think it's like one of two stoplights on the whole island. There was a yoga and Rolfing studio across from where we were sitting in the car. In a town of 8,000 people on an island in Alaska, seeing that there was a Rolfer was my sign.

I started getting Rolfing and I started yoga. I started feeling better. It didn't cure my pain, but it definitely helped. It helped so much that I wanted to become a Rolfer myself so that I could help others with their pain. I could see the benefits. I could see the need for Rolfing, also known as structural integration, and I could see the value and what it would provide, so I became a Rolfer.

In clients, I noticed imbalances of strength from the sides of the body, so I became a certified personal trainer as well. However, the reality was, something was still off with me. I wasn't fully out of pain or sadness. By this point I had already removed myself cold turkey from all medications.

I kept hearing about food making a different in people's pain, and while I thought they were crazy, I started to research and study it. It wasn't long before I realized the impact of food on my body and I noticed the same for people that I was working with. I started studying more about food healing.

At some point, I recognized you can eat the healthiest foods you could, work out till your heart is content, have a structurally aligned body, and you can still be very sick, in pain and even have cancer or other diseases. It was clear to me, that the mind was more powerful than anything else. I became an Integrative Nutrition Health Coach and started health coaching.

However, I recognized in my conversations, people still wanted a pill they could take for a quick fix. They weren't interested in learning and didn't want to change their mindset or lifestyle. I recognized that if that's the client that I'm attracting, then I have some deeper work that I need to do. I started diving deep into personal development, taking radical responsibility for myself and my life. I decided in the meantime that I needed to switch careers, so that I could focus on my healing and make an income at the same time. I became a Licensed Real Estate professional and continued to work on myself on the side.

When I look back over my journey and all the healing, it's clear there are multiple layers, just like an onion. Each time I peeled off a layer, another appeared. There's no pill to fix things. Sometimes when I look back, I think, "Oh my goodness, if it has taken me all these years, all this amount of money, and all of this time, how in the world can we expect anybody to heal?" The reality is it doesn't have to take that long. I just did it the hard way. It is part of my journey to be able to share with you and if you're reading this book there's something in here for you.

I'm a firm believer that there's no bad or wrong healer or healing experience. I can look back and ask why I wasted all of this time doing XYZ when now I have access to a new level of healing that I didn't have before. I can regret all the time and money I thought I wasted; however, I firmly believe that I wouldn't be where I am now and wouldn't have the results that I have now, had I not gone through those experiences and had those healings. Each healing and experience opened me up and prepared me for a new level, a new layer. There is always either something to be learned while a layer is shed or a new upgrade from each and every experience.

Nina is originally from Lawrence, Kansas and moved to Florida in 1998 while in college when her family relocated to Bradenton, Florida. She graduated from the University of Tampa with a B.S. in Finance. In 2001, she was commissioned into the U.S. Army and served as a Finance Officer for just over 7 years, serving overseas in South Korea and completed a Combat tour in Iraq. She honorably ended her term of service in 2008. She feels her purpose in this life is as a healer and messenger, empowering others to connect more fully to themselves, our creator and others, in order to heal themselves. Nina experienced many years of feeling helpless and lifeless and she now embraces and wants to feel alive and truly live and help others do the same.

Nina became a Certified Rolfer, Licensed Massage Therapist, Certified Personal Trainer, Certified Integrative Nutrition Health Coach, Certified Corporate Wellness Specialist, Yoga Instructor, Reike Master, Certified Emotion Code Practitioner, and Certified Body Code Practitioner on her journey to heal and in return assist others on their journey. Nina is currently undergoing certification to become an Emotional Energetic Release Therapist (Breathwork) and a Holographic Manipulation Therapist, as well as an Educator of Germanic Heilkunde (Germanic New Medicine).

theselfhealingcollaborative@gmail.com
https://www.facebook.com/groups/selfhealingcollaborative

Chapter Seven
From Survival to Freedom
By Carla Center

*Real Transformation requires real honesty.
If you want to move forward-
get real with yourself!*
-Brian McGill

This chapter will take you with me on my own healing journey as well as show you some of the amazing results my clients have experienced due to us working together. It will also show you what services I offer.

The starts, stops, and challenges that ultimately guided me on the path that brought me to the place I am today. I'm a heart centered, intuitive healer who guides and supports clients as they walk along their own healing path to create the life they want and love.

I grew up in a household much like my friends that surrounded me. I was the oldest of three and had two hardworking parents that had married young but did everything they could to give their children a good life. We were kids of the 70s and 80s. If schoolwork and chores were done, we were outside somewhere with friends playing and riding bikes until dinner or dark whichever came first.

From the outside I was an intelligent, kind girl destined to accomplish anything I set my mind to now. On the inside, I was a scared little girl terrified of upsetting those I cared about and anyone finding out about the things that had happened to me. I also didn't want the imperfections that didn't align with that perfect, obedient child I portrayed to be seen. I was sure if anyone truly knew who I was even my parents they wouldn't love me. I was outgoing with those I knew and trusted and shy and reserved with those I didn't know or trust.

So, I started my healing journey at the age of 16. My abuser had passed away the year before and I was at a school assembly where there was a play done by a group of teens and a non-profit meant to help teens experiencing physical or sexual abuse to reach out for help. I had never told anyone because I was afraid, I had done something wrong to cause it.

The school counselor helped me tell my mom who helped me find a psychologist. I wanted to release the pain however I did not want to do the things this counselor asked of me. To shift from behaviors that had served my survival all these years was not what I wanted.

I wanted someone to listen to me not tell me how to be assertive. I was comfortable with my dual personality. Only showing who I was to certain people and being that quiet, smart, good girl for everyone else. Having boundaries and possibly conflict terrified me. So, I quit counseling pretty quickly.

I joined a confidential support group at school for others that had experienced sexual abuse. I got my story out in a two-page anonymous article in the high school newspaper encouraging others to find a way to heal. Being one of the editors of the newspaper allowed me to work with the teacher to make this happen.

That's when I decided I was going to be a healer and I was going to do whatever I needed to heal others that felt like they were never going to be loved or be enough. I didn't want anyone to feel like I felt. I wanted to heal the world.

At age 17, I volunteered for a local non-profit that had many different programs that supported clients needing an array of social services. I chose to work for the Helpline program. I received training in many different things including suicide prevention and guiding people to the resources available in our area. For the most part I loved the time I volunteered. The one suicide call scared me but what I enjoyed most was the connection and helping others have a more joyous life. I had no idea I was about to make choices to keep me in this same space. My pattern was as I was on the verge of true change, I would sabotage it.

I became pregnant my senior year in high school and graduated high school 7 months pregnant. I kept my mask of being the smart good girl and graduated in the top 10% of my class. I never shared how terrified I was of being a mom and not knowing how I was going to be a healer and a good mom.

It would take me until the age of 21 to be ready for my next step in my healing journey. I had just gotten married and thought, "I don't want to be the mom that works crazy hours, and my daughter is raised by daycare while I work late and on weekends." My husband also worked retail and I thought I get to make this my opportunity to become a psychologist.

So, I applied and got enrolled in the psychology program at Southern Oregon University. The program was not just about theories and learning but truly doing self-work and my favorite classes challenged me and made me look within. My senior year, they decided to redesign the Master of Counseling degree and I had to change my plans.

Fresh out of college with a Bachelor of Science in Psychology I was looking for a way to get experience and not go back to retail. I found a position as an AmeriCorps Member with the Reduce Adolescent Pregnancy Project. I got to work with so many different programs in my community that year and even create my own program to fill a gap where I saw a group of teen girls that were falling through the cracks.

I truly felt like I was making a difference. That was my beginning of working with non-profits, churches and government agencies making a difference in my community. However, I still wasn't addressing the issue I'm not lovable, I'm not enough. I just kept pouring out to others and not looking for ways to heal my own stuff.

Then as I was turning 30, I was struggling with health issues, overwhelmed by the state of my marriage and my career. Within that year I found myself divorced, pregnant with my third child, jobless, homeless, and feeling hopeless. The next year I got myself back on my feet, had a job, an apartment, a stable job and three amazing kids. I went into total survival mode. Never acknowledging all that I over came in that year only the feelings of being a victim of all the things that got me to where I had been the year before.

I found my health deteriorating and my relationships being distant and not very authentic. I had learned how to be everyone's best friend and not allowed anyone close enough to truly be my friend. I tried counselors but we always went down the path of me getting my PHD.

I just didn't feel like as a single mom that was possible especially with the medical bills. I went down the traditional medicine route, naturopathic medicine, acupuncture, supplements, and all the different things I could find. I had bad anxiety, depression, and had been diagnosed with Rheumatoid Arthritis.

I had gotten to the point that besides things required of me I just wanted to be in bed hiding from the world. Two of my kids were grown and my youngest was in high school. I had given up on myself. I had spent 30+ years supporting and guiding others but couldn't find a way to help myself.

May 1, 2021 was the day I found a missing piece that I needed to not only become a better healer but also to heal myself. I had been told two weeks earlier by my friend and mentor Rebecca Blust about this workshop she was going to present at titled The Best Self-Development Workshop on Earth. She said I needed to go as the main presenter Dr. Gabe Roberts said he could guide you to release traumas in 2 minutes.

I did not sign up right away in fact I didn't register until 11 hours before it began. I could barely get out of bed unless I was going to work or doing the required things to keep my household afloat. How was someone going to help me get past all the deaths and tragedies the previous 2.5 years is what I kept telling myself. As you notice I still wasn't acknowledging the childhood stuff I used to judge myself on. My final decision came down to how much I truly trust and respect Rebecca.

That first day made such an impact on me that I said out loud that when the school began, I wanted to become certified in HMT. I hadn't turned on my camera or even spoken in the Zoom workshop. I had just followed Dr. Robert's instructions on doing a Holographic Deletion.

That one technique had relieved my anxiety in a way that none of the traditional medicine, acupuncture, naturopathic or supplements had done. I used Holographic Deletion again when those anxiety feelings came up, but I didn't have to do it very often after that first time. I had something in my toolbox that I could easily use on myself, and I was so excited.

A month later I was studying to be an HMT Therapist. I was well on my journey to being pain free and no longer taking medicine for my Rheumatoid Arthritis and having similar results for my clients. I have had amazing results with clients and my own healing that I didn't think was possible. I no longer take any medications and can move freely in ways that haven't been possible in about 5 years.

As I did my training, I finally was addressing the parts of me that kept me living as that scared little girl my whole life. As I released each moment of overwhelm, I found myself searching out new ways to grow as those filters that showed me I wasn't enough, I wouldn't be loved started disappearing. My relationships are stronger and are now authentic as I have no reason to wear a mask anymore and pretend to be someone I am not. I am now living a life I love while guiding other women through their healing journey to do the same.

Client Cases

I am going to share the stories of some of my most recent clients and the amazing result they have had working with me. Names will not be shared for privacy purposes, and I have gotten permission to share these stories.

First, we have a hard-working mother of two in her mid-thirties that struggled with neck, shoulder, and carpal tunnel pain. She had tried, traditional medicine, massage therapy, chiropractic, and natural remedies. All worked temporarily.

Before she went to the next step of having surgery, she wanted to try working with me doing HMT. Each session her pain got better and after a few sessions she was pain free. I didn't have her take any supplements or do any physical work on her. We merely found the moments of overwhelm that were trapped in her body and reframed and released them.

We found long forgotten memories that had caused her to feel abandoned, unwanted, scared and like she had no control. We reframed these in a way that she got exactly what she needed to feel whole and like she didn't have the unconscious need to keep replaying those moments to keep her safe. It has been more than a year and she continues to be pain free. She was holding these childhood traumas in, and they were coming out as physical pain in her body.

Here is her testimonial:

"My experience with Carla was absolutely incredible. I have dealt with shoulder pain for the last several years. I've seen a variety of providers for treatment: massage therapists, chiropractors, and my general physician. I have relied on muscle relaxers, constant stretching, CBD balms help ease the daily pain. Never would I have thought that my mind and emotional pain was contributing to this physically debilitating shoulder pain. After just two

sessions with Carla, I woke up one morning and the pain was gone, my body is so much more relaxed and my mind more at peace. No matter what you might be suffering from I believe whole heartedly in this provider and what she can pull to the forefront physically, emotionally, and mentally to bring to you a new level of wellness."

A 7-year-old boy that was diagnosed with ADHD and being on the autism spectrum. His mom brought him to me as he was getting messages sent home daily from the teacher complaining about all the things, he wasn't doing right during the school day. He was sad and trying his best. She was exhausted and not sure what more she could do for him. He had all the resources at school, and she was doing all the things she knew to do that would support him.

After the first session he had a week where the teacher had one complaint that his happy squeal could have been at a better time. We did sessions weekly for a month and his school year went better and he no longer got bad reports. This year he has had great success at school. He is flourishing in his learning, and if he needs to clear out his field, I can guide him quickly over the phone.

Next is a woman suffering from an auto-immune disorder. She was exhausted, struggling with pain, anxiety and unable to do the things she wanted to do not only for herself but with her family. She wasn't feeling like herself and was struggling with how

isolated she felt due to the pain, anger and other things that kept her at home and unable to enjoy her life.
In the months we worked together we found traumas in her childhood that she wasn't even aware of that were contributing to her pain and isolation. As her health improved after our sessions, she was able to walk 2 miles 1-2 times daily eventually getting to go out on family outings.

Most of the memories she wasn't consciously aware of and even contacted her mom to confirm some moments. Her mom didn't remember a pattern on the couch matching what the client had described but when she found a picture of it the pattern described by the client was an exact match. As she healed her physical health improved. It was an absolute pleasure watching her transformation over the months we worked together.

Her testimonial:
"I had such an amazing transformation and I'm so grateful. I wish it was possible to continue but I do believe I now have the tools to keep going myself! I had the best experience with Carla. She made me feel safe and comfortable and we have a lot in common. I'm already sending people your way! Thank for the experience. It's been truly life changing for my entire family! What you do is so extraordinary, and it has saved my life!"

A 23-year-old young woman came to me with neck and shoulder pain that she had been suffering from since a car accident she was in 8 years previously. As we were doing our session she would stop and stretch it out. She would catch herself stretching often and even with working with massage therapists and chiropractors it still continued to get tight.

As we did our session and did different HMT techniques the tightness released. She was in awe that clearing the field and reframing the memory that trapped her shoulder had done what she's been unable to do all those years. As I've watched her in videos and posts over the last 18 months moving freely and with joy, I smile knowing her shoulder is better and she's free of the pain she was holding on to.

My last case I will share with you is a very successful businesswoman. She puts her whole heart and soul into her business but still felt the need to earn her worthiness. She would do for others to the point of exhaustion and not truly take in her accomplishments.

The cycle was wearing her down and she was ready to make changes to find a way that worked better for her. After one session she called me and said she felt a sense of empowerment and standing in her own power that she hadn't felt before. She was no longer making decisions based on what she expected other's reaction to be or out of needing to earn others approval. She is flourishing in her business and is a true leader. She does things now based on her dreams and goals not based on earning her worth.

These cases are a taste of the transformations I've seen.

Testimonials:

Working with Carla has been a fantastic experience. I came to her with a problem of not know what it was really about. I was confused and hurt. I was crying for everything and anything. During the session with Carla, she calmed me down, helped me connect deeply and listen openly. Then she stared to ask me questions and guided me through the process she applies. It was a magical journey. She took me through a healing journey where I was able to safely touch on my emotions and events related to them and release from its conception.

She was sweet and supportive throughout the process and even gave me tools to continue my healing journey. She cared about my well-being above all. I highly recommend her therapies and working with her. I really appreciate her support, professionalism, thoughtfulness and dedication! -Lorena

Working with Carla has been like walking into a 360 degree canvas of my life, transforming stories from my past to include the beauty, wisdom and creativity in them that were once overshadowed with pain. With Carla I immediate felt relaxed, calm, and safe to explore even the most painful experiences. Carla is kind, calm, loving, confident and humble. I know I could bring any topic to Carla, and it would be held with care. –JR

When it comes to working with Carla, she is very attentive, compassionate, non-judgmental, and loving. The work she is doing is HUGE! It's helped me with body pain I never knew how to reach and helped me transmute the trauma & anxieties that have been stored. I never knew of this type of work, and I'm so glad Carla was my first! She's so gentle and guides me through deep parts of myself while holding a deep safe container!! Which is so soo soooo important! Carla is bubbly and fully of light, she never fails to check in on me after a session AND continues to make sure I'm doing good still! I really appreciated all the love and healing she gives and guides others through and I love her!!!! -Zola

In one session with Carla my back pain that I have been suffering with for years decreased by 80%! Working with her has made a huge difference in my life! -MM

Carla's work is amazing! She expertly guided me through a healing of some traumatic dreams and memories that I've had since I was a very young girl. By clearing the emotions around them and reimagining them, I now get to live with the feeling of being protected by the trees and the animals in the most beautiful, magical way!!! -CS

I had an amazingly transformative healing session with Carla. Her energy and empathy is so beautiful. I felt so loved and connected with myself after it was over. I feel like I really healed parts of my fragmented soul that I had dissociated from due to childhood trauma. -Kelly

Working with Carla, I immediate felt safe and see, opening me up to surprise about where the direction of our session took. With Carla's loving guidance and skill, I created a beautiful fresh context about the story of my birth. The impact of this one session continues to ripple in my life. It is a treasure to work with Carla who is so clearly committed to holding an authentic and loving space. -Julie

What I offer

I work with women who are looking to move from just making it through life to creating the life they want. I have 1-month, 3-month and 6-month programs to support the needs of different clients. I will guide and support you as you pursue the life you've always wanted but felt that something has been holding you back.

We will release trauma and moments of overwhelm that have been stored in your body. There have been roadblocks and limiting beliefs that keep you in a cycle and have not allowed you to level up to the place you want to be in life. We will work together to get you to where you want to be not just to where you have settled for due to feeling hopeless, exhausted, or lost on how to move forward on your path. I combined my skills, experience, and gifts to give you a program tailored for your needs and wants. I am certified in HMT, Life Coaching, Mindset, and many other modalities.

We start out with a consultation so we can get to know each other and to see if what I have to offer is right for you. We will create a daily routine that you can do easily that will support you in shifting your life in this new direction. There will be weekly sessions with me that will support you and guide you as you move forward. For those that feel they no longer want/need weekly guidance at the end of their contract can sign up for the maintenance program where we meet monthly and work on new goals or anything else that has come up during the month.

Tips

- Invest in yourself physically, spiritually, and emotionally not just financially. For true transformation you must be invested in your own self-development. No matter how amazing the healer or their modality is without your investment it won't get you the results you want in the time you are expecting.
- Daily self-care like a morning routine that is less than 15 minutes long is not selfish and is a good reminder that you matter. Like they say on the airplanes before we take off you must help yourself before you are able to help someone else.
- Gratitude daily will help you with opening your eyes to the positive things in your life.
- Connect with nature as much as possible.

- Be present in your conversations with others. When we multi-task and don't listen to understand, then misunderstandings and frustrations happen.
- Being open to new experiences makes more things possible in our future.
- Don't quit or beat yourself up over perceived mistakes or failures.
- Trust your intuition

Carla not only has the knowledge and skills it requires to be an amazing HMT therapist, but also the heart and gifts that support clients in achieving amazing results. She has a doctorate in Metaphysics, bachelor's in psychology and is certified I multiple disciplines in addition to HMT. Carla has guided and supported hundreds of clients in finding the root cause and out of living a life of just survival. Since her teens has pursued her passion for helping others. As she was on her own healing journey and felt that she just couldn't find anything that would help, she found HMT Therapy. After her first HMT experience, she decided to shift from Social work to become an HMT Therapist.

You can contact me by emailing me at carlathehealer@gmail.com or by DM on Facebook (Carla Ragsdale-Center) or Instagram (carlaragsdalecenter)

Chapter Eight

Embracing the Journey

As we reach the end of our shared exploration in "The Way to Wholeness," it is essential to reflect on the journey we've taken together. Throughout the previous chapters, we have delved into the realms of self-discovery, healing, and growth. We've learned about the power of mindfulness, the significance of emotional intelligence, and the importance of compassion and empathy in our relationships with others. We've investigated the impact of our thoughts, beliefs, and habits on our well-being, and we have strived to cultivate resilience and adaptability in the face of life's inevitable challenges.

This closing chapter is an opportunity to pause and take stock of the progress you have made on your path to wholeness. It's also a chance to celebrate the small victories along the way, to acknowledge the hard work and commitment required for personal transformation.

Finally, it is a time to recognize that the journey to wholeness is never truly complete; it is an ongoing process of growth, self-awareness, and evolution that will continue throughout our lives.

The importance of reflection and celebration

Reflection and celebration are essential components of our journey to wholeness. Taking the time to reflect on our experiences and progress allows us to gain valuable insights into our own personal growth. It helps us recognize patterns, understand our motivations, and make connections between seemingly disparate aspects of our lives. It also offers an opportunity to integrate our newfound knowledge and wisdom into our daily existence.

Celebrating our achievements, no matter how small or seemingly insignificant, is crucial for maintaining motivation and momentum on our path. Every step we take, every challenge we overcome, and every insight we gain is worth acknowledging and honoring. In doing so, we cultivate a sense of gratitude and appreciation for the journey itself and reinforce the belief that we are capable of growth and transformation.

The journey is the destination.

It's essential to recognize that the journey to wholeness is not a finite process with a clear beginning and end. Rather, it is an ongoing, ever-evolving pursuit that will continue throughout our lives. As we grow, learn, and change, so too will our understanding of ourselves and the world around us. This constant evolution is a testament to the limitless potential of the human spirit and our capacity for self-discovery and growth.

As we move forward on our path, we may encounter new challenges, setbacks, and obstacles. However, these moments are not failures or indications that we have lost our way. Instead, they are opportunities for growth, learning, and increased self-awareness. The journey to wholeness is, in many ways, a series of lessons and experiences designed to help us continually evolve and expand our understanding of ourselves and the world around us.

Embracing the unknown

One of the key aspects of the journey to wholeness is embracing the unknown. As we delve deeper into our own personal growth and transformation, we may find ourselves facing unfamiliar territory or confronting aspects of ourselves that we have long ignored or denied. This can be uncomfortable, challenging, and at times, even frightening. However, it is precisely in these moments of uncertainty and vulnerability that we have the opportunity to make the most significant strides in our personal growth.

Embracing the unknown requires courage, resilience, and a willingness to let go of our preconceived notions and beliefs. It is an act of surrender, a recognition that we do not have all the answers and that the journey is as much about unlearning as it is about learning. By relinquishing our attachment to certainty and control, we open ourselves up to the possibility of growth and transformation in ways we may never have imagined.

Cultivating gratitude and compassion

As we continue our path to wholeness, it is essential to cultivate a sense of gratitude and compassion for ourselves and others. Gratitude allows us to appreciate the present moment and the gifts that life has to offer. It helps us recognize the beauty and abundance that surrounds us and fosters a deep sense of connection to the world and the people in it. By practicing gratitude, we develop a greater sense of contentment and satisfaction, which can be invaluable in maintaining our motivation and enthusiasm on our journey to wholeness.

Compassion is equally important, as it serves as a reminder that we are all interconnected and that our individual struggles and triumphs are, in many ways, shared experiences. Cultivating compassion for ourselves is essential in recognizing that we, too, are deserving of love, kindness, and understanding. It allows us to extend the same level of empathy and support to ourselves that we offer to others, fostering a sense of self-acceptance and self-love that is crucial for personal growth and transformation.

In extending compassion to others, we deepen our connections and strengthen our relationships, creating a supportive and nurturing environment in which we can continue to grow and evolve. By practicing compassion, we also recognize the humanity in others and ourselves, fostering a sense of unity and interconnectedness that is vital to our overall well-being.

Moving forward with courage and resilience

As we close this chapter and continue on our journey to wholeness, it's essential to approach each new day with courage and resilience. This means acknowledging that growth and transformation may not always be easy or comfortable, but they are necessary for our ongoing evolution and self-discovery.

Facing our fears, embracing the unknown, and persevering in the face of adversity requires determination, persistence, and an unwavering belief in our own inherent strength and resilience. By cultivating these qualities within ourselves, we equip ourselves with the tools necessary to navigate the twists and turns of life and to continue moving forward with purpose and intention.

In conclusion

The journey to wholeness is a lifelong pursuit, one that requires patience, dedication, and a willingness to embrace the many challenges and opportunities that life presents. As you continue to explore your own path to wholeness, remember that the journey itself is the destination, and that every step along the way is an opportunity for growth, self-discovery, and transformation.

Take the time to reflect on your progress, celebrate your achievements, and honor the work you have done thus far. Embrace the unknown with courage and curiosity and cultivate gratitude and compassion for yourself and others. And above all, trust in your own resilience and the limitless potential of your spirit.

As you move forward on your path to wholeness, may you continue to grow, learn, and evolve, ever mindful of the beauty and wonder that resides within you and the world around you.

Remember that you are never alone on this journey. Surround yourself with a supportive community of like-minded individuals who share your goals and aspirations for growth and wholeness. Lean on one another for encouragement, wisdom, and inspiration, and offer the same in return. The connections we make and the relationships we cultivate are invaluable sources of strength and sustenance as we navigate the complexities of life.

It's also important to recognize that personal growth and transformation do not exist in a vacuum. Our journey to wholeness is deeply intertwined with our relationships to others, the environment, and the world at large. By acknowledging and embracing our interconnectedness, we are better equipped to foster positive change not only within ourselves but also within our communities and beyond.

As you continue your path, remain open to new experiences, ideas, and perspectives. Recognize that everyone you encounter has something unique and valuable to offer and that there is always more to learn and discover. Be willing to challenge your own beliefs and assumptions, and strive to cultivate an open, curious, and non-judgmental mindset. This openness will enable you to grow and evolve in ways that are both unexpected and profound.

Take care of yourself physically, mentally, and emotionally. Prioritize self-care and self-compassion, recognizing that nurturing our own well-being is essential for our ability to grow and thrive. Develop practices that nourish and replenish your mind, body, and spirit, and make a conscious effort to maintain balance and harmony in your life.

And finally, as you traverse the path to wholeness, always remember to pause and appreciate the beauty and wonder of the present moment. Life is a precious, fleeting gift, and it is in the present that we have the opportunity to experience the full depth and breadth of its riches. Cultivate mindfulness, presence, and gratitude, and allow these qualities to infuse every aspect of your life with a sense of joy, wonder, and awe.

As this book comes to a close, it's essential to remember that your journey to wholeness is uniquely yours. The path you choose, the experiences you encounter, and the lessons you learn along the way are all part of the intricate tapestry of your life. Embrace the complexity and the nuance, the triumphs and the challenges, and trust that each step you take is contributing to your growth, evolution, and ultimate wholeness.

May the insights and wisdom shared within these pages serve as a guide and inspiration as you continue on your path. May you find the courage to face your fears, the resilience to overcome adversity, and the compassion to connect with others. And above all, may your journey to wholeness be filled with love, light, and boundless possibility.

One Last Message

Dear Reader,

As we part ways, we want to leave you with a heartfelt message of encouragement and hope. Remember that the journey you embark on with "The Way to Wholeness" is a deeply personal and transformative one, with each step bringing you closer to the person you strive to become.

Throughout this journey, be gentle with yourself, for growth and transformation take time and patience. Embrace the challenges that lie ahead and recognize that they are opportunities for self-discovery and growth. You are capable of incredible change, and your potential for wholeness knows no bounds.

Never forget that you are a unique and irreplaceable being, an essential part of the intricate web of life. Your experiences, insights, and wisdom have the power to touch others in profound and meaningful ways. Share your light with the world, and in doing so, you will inspire others to embark on their own journeys toward wholeness.

As you continue to evolve, remember to carry with you the lessons and insights from this book. They will serve as a compass, guiding you through the challenges and triumphs that await you. May your journey be filled with love, compassion, and a deep sense of purpose, and may you always find joy in the process of growth and self-discovery.

With warmest wishes for a life of wholeness and fulfillment,

Dr Tiffany Roberts

> Go and wake up your luck!"
> -Persian Proverb

ULTIMATE SELF-DEVELOPMENT COURSE
https://freegiftfromshm.com/

ABOUT THE ROBERTS

Dr Tiffany Roberts the Founder of Holographic Manipulation Therapy and is a NLP Practitioner, Certified Clinical Hypnotherapist, Self-sabotage coach, has a master's in nutrition, Doctorate in Metaphysics and is completing her PhD with Quantum University as a Doctor of Natural Medicine. She is an author, homeschooling mom of a beautiful 7-year-old daughter and is a Master of Essential Oil application for therapeutic uses. Her specialty is working with woman and children in releasing traumas and repressed emotions hindering the optimal potential within.

Dr Gabe Roberts is a Holographic Manipulation Therapist, Clinical Hypnotherapist, NLP Practitioner, Quantum Integration Practitioner, has a Doctorate in Metaphysics, he holds a Doctorate in Chiropractic and is Certified in Functional Medicine. is a specialist of psychosomatic illnesses including autoimmune conditions, chronic pain, chronic fatigue, digestive illnesses, neurological conditions, depression and a host of mystery conditions that have at their root cause repressed emotions.

www.thesubconscioushealer.com

ADDITIONAL RESOURCES

IGNITE YOUR FIRE

IGNITE THE FIRE WITHIN YOU AND START THE HEALING PROCESS TODAY

https://thesubconscious healer.com/ignite-your-fire

THE VAULT

ACCESS ALL OUR COURSES AND LECTURES FOR ONE YEAR

https://thesubconscious healer.com/the-vault

www.ingramcontent.com/pod-product-compliance
Lightning Source LLC
Chambersburg PA
CBHW060030180426
43196CB00044B/2282